Praise for Loved:

In John 4:12 Jesus said to the Samaritan woman, "Everyone who drinks this water will be thirsty again, **14** but whoever drinks the water I give them will never thirst. Indeed, the water I give them will become in them a spring of water welling up to eternal life."

Love is the essence of Life; we all need it, desire it and work very hard to find it. Without love we have nothing; with it we have life. This book is a true revelation of the journey and the paths we take to find only what Jesus can really provide. Just as Jesus stated, we all have a thirst, but that thirst can never be satisfied by other humans, possessions, or accomplishments. Most of us have the wrong idea of what perfect love really is. This book is an eye-opener in the way that it points out what many of us believe love truly is. If you read this book and really meditate on the truth, you will find healing and true redirection, allowing that healing to make love truly possible again. This book has given me the desire to encounter Christ even deeper and given me hope that Love is truly possible for all, even the ones that are broken and bitter. This book is for all readers because we all need Love. All of us have those voids in our life because we have heavily relied on temporary, imperfect things that have satisfied us for a time but were no longer present. As you read this book, you will be able to recognize those voids and replace them with the living and breathing truth. In my experience, I have come across many that have had a broken relationship with their earthly father, the harsh reality of that experience has left them with the idea that God is an angry, finger-pointing, and judgmental God. A God that in all of our efforts is disappointed and not satisfied with us. This book allows you to see how we compare God the father with our earthly father and how we can open our eyes to truly see the character of God... Love. I recommend this book because I believe it will challenge you to seek a love that will never leave you thirsty again."

—**Deborahan Queen**, speaker; minister; revivalist at *AwakeAmerica365*.

***

This book takes you on a deep quest of God's most basic, most powerful, and most personal attribute, Love. Through this poetic prophetic path, you will not only answer the question of who Love is but experience what Love has done for you. As you encounter Him on the raw and rugged journey that is held not only within these pages, but also within your heart, may you truly grasp Love's width and length, height, and depth, and never be the same.

—**Tiffany Jo Baker**, speaker; podcaster; author of *Soul-Care for Go-Getters.*

***

Through these pages, you will be taken on a beautiful journey of healing and experience God in a beautiful new way. Anna's words paint a beautiful story of an encounter with our Heavenly Father and His perfect love. Her creativity and descriptive words immerse you into the beauty of creation. You will be transformed by these intimate visuals of closeness with God. I pray they pierce your heart with a new revelation of His goodness and His reckless love for you! This book is a gift to all who will read it! You are about to be so blessed by what you're holding in your hand.

—**Marissa McCrory**, speaker; minister; coach; founder of *Soul Prosper.*

***

Whether you are already lovesick for Jesus or don't know Him at all, *Loved* is a prophetic journey that will find you falling more in love with the Lover of your Soul. This tale of divine intimacy captivates the heart of the reader with the heart of the Creator by exploring the often-unseen realities of spiritual warfare. Frail humanity is met with mercy, changed by grace, and sealed with a love like no other. Activate your imagination and experience new realms of freedom as you encounter Him afresh within the pages of **Loved**.

— **Janice Rigel**, speaker; podcaster, author of *Slayin' Singlehood*.

***

Loved is an adventure from cover to cover. Once you step into this world full of mystery and enchantment with Love by your side, you will not want to leave!

—**Briana Richardson**, musician; artist; writer

LOVED

A Mountain Moving Encounter

with the God of Love

Anna Pranger

Published by KHARIS PUBLISHING, imprint of KHARIS MEDIA LLC.

Copyright © 2021 Anna Pranger

ISBN-13: 978-1-63746-032-0

ISBN-10: 1-63746-032-5

Library of Congress Control Number: 2021935800

All KHARIS PUBLISHING products are available at special quantity discounts for bulk purchase for sales promotions, premiums, fund-raising, and educational needs. For details, contact:

Kharis Media LLC
Tel: 1-479-599-8657
support@kharispublishing.com
www.kharispublishing.com

TABLE OF CONTENTS

Acknowledgement

I want to thank my parents, grandparents, siblings and family for their continued love and support as they encourage me on this journey. There is nothing more powerful than the love and support of family

In loving memory of my cousins Gracie and Max, and my Uncle Roger. They are my heavenly family who have taught me what living is truly about. Their lives continue to impact many people as they spur us on to find and pursue God's love and goodness.

May we never forget to display God's love and goodness in all that we do for as long as we are here on earth.

Prologue

Who is Love? Is Love a person, a feeling, or an entity that can be obtained? Is it a creative expression that paints the sky and breathes life into stagnant organs forcing a gentle steady beat? Who caused our brains to communicate to our legs and gave our minds the power to form thoughts? Who delicately traced the cells of our body causing them to form together, creating a flesh being? Who formed the soul made up of our will and emotions to gaze at the rustling of trees and yearn for someone we cannot see? The answer? Love: a creative energy who formed you in your mother's womb and spoke to the moon and stars. Yes, Love, who created your mind and counted the hairs on your head. Yes, Love, a being who desired to be with you in the wholeness of relationship.

Without Love, we find emptiness, yearning, and a pit of loneliness as we self-medicate, isolate, and create mind traps to feel okay. Those places of darkness that even those who know us most cannot see. Those places are not hidden but seen by an energy of Love that cannot be felt with the touch of a nerve. What if I told you that the darkest places in your mind can be changed to wholeness through one tiny ray of light? What if I told you that the emptiness you feel, that has created the shell of a person you are, can be filled with a tangible substance? What if the light not only exposes the darkness but also makes the screeching thoughts of fear go silent? Love can calm the raging storms of your mind as He silences the fear with one gaze. Love can shine the light in the darkness and eradicate the demons as they flee in terror. Love can captivate your soul and bring life back to the broken places of your heart. No self-medication or protective mechanism is lasting; you will always go back for more. But Love can make you whole. From everlasting to everlasting, He is God. (Psalm 90:2)

I am sorry that religion made you feel as if you were not good enough. I am sorry that self-proclaimed "Christians" told you that your sin was "too dirty," and your secrets should be held in the *shame cage* called bondage and condemnation, forcing you to act more out of fear than the wholeness that you were called to.

I am sorry you were told that you were too rigid and unfiltered for systematic believers. I am sorry that you were stoned by sinners instead of being met with eyes of Love that knelt in the dust and wrote, "you who have not sinned throw the first stone." I am sorry that twisting of scripture caused you so much pain as self-proclaimed "teachers" threw insults your way, convincing you that your past would never be viewed as redeemable. I am sorry that prideful Pharisees crept in and tore you to pieces as you were told, "if only you had faith, if only you believed," making you feel like even God Himself turned His back on you.

I am sorry for the violation of your space, as innocence was ripped from you by the man or woman who acted one way in the light and entirely different in the darkness of your bedroom. I am sorry that someone hurt you so badly that it caused you pain and destruction, and you rejected the idea of a loving God--or a God at all.

Your experiences may have caused you to believe in a God of anger or judgement. Maybe you have completely rejected the idea of God because of the fallen state of our world. Or maybe you do believe in God and even in a God of Love. Wherever you are in your journey, this book will unveil the truth that has been buried beneath the lies that you have believed and the hurt you have endured. I pray that you will heal from the rejection you have faced as you forgive those who have thrown stones. Though you may have been rejected, it is crucial that you do not reject the Creator of your soul. I ask that you read this journey in its entirety with an open mind and an active imagination.

I believe that you will find peace in your heart as the truth of God is revealed as a person of Love. My friends, those self-proclaimed "Christians" who hurt you--they were not God. Those who rejected you--they were not God. And those who abused you--they were not God. No matter the condition of your soul, one thing is obvious: we all need a Savior. We all need a Love to fill the deep void within us. Nothing in or on this earth will satisfy our needs, nothing will fill the void, except the person of Love. All I ask is that you give Him a chance. Consider this as an invitation from the One who is relentlessly in pursuit of your healing and true freedom. As you continue to pick up this book, you may battle with reading these words. I encourage you to allow the word "Jesus" to fall off your lips as you ask for help to continue this journey.

Allow your imagination to see yourself in the throne room of God. He wants you to ask the hard questions because, unlike the world, He has the answers. With a bit of endurance and a tiny ounce of faith, let us begin our journey of discovering the person of Love.

Chapter One

Who is Love?

The Lord your God is in your midst, a mighty one who will save; he will rejoice over you with gladness; he will quiet you by his love; he will exult over you with loud singing. —Zephaniah 3:17

Hello, my child, the one whom I have desired, the one whom I created. Allow me to introduce myself: I Am Love. I knew you in your Mother's womb, I sought you before you were even a thought, I desired you when you were merely a cell. I turned the eyes of the universe upon you the day I heard your first whimper. I may be getting ahead of myself; we have truly just met. You see, I know everything about you; I know the hairs on your head. I know your quirks and the way you process thoughts. I know this because I created these things. I want you to experience the level of Love that I have for you. I created the earth, a perfect haven for you to make your home. From the beginning of time, I desired a relationship with you and will do everything in my perfect power to get you back to my original idea--a glorified union with me.

I will keep your attention as I journey with you through the mountaintops and valleys. Knowing me is knowing yourself. Step by step with me you will discover your true identity and the very reason you were created. Within me you will be convinced of my divinity as your mind grasps that I truly know you.

People are fed lies about me. My exact opposite named Hate runs rampant in this fallen world you call home. I have made my existence known and obvious, but one thing stops many from having eyes to see and ears to hear: hate. Before I get into exposing the lies, I first need you to trust me.

I want to take you on a journey. Grab my hand. I will not fail you; I will not hurt you. I know you have been hurt before. I know your trust has been broken, but with me it is different, and I will prove it. Now, hand in hand, imagine with me. You are safe for just a moment and all fear and anxiety leaves; the hate is silenced, and the hurt in this world is frozen. You are safe, say it out loud, feel it in your heart. Let the peace of that knowledge wash over you: you are safe. Now follow me.

The breeze is cool, and the sun is warm on your face. You can feel your hand in mine. I guide you along the top ridge of an open canyon. The rocks beneath you are sturdy as you are guided along by my hand. You follow closely behind me. The leaves rustle in the wind and the birds fly overhead. I guide you to the side of the canyon and we sit. Our legs dangle off the side as we swing them together in perfect rhythm. I place my hand on your heart, and you turn your head and look into my eyes. You see fire and I see fear. "Be a brave child, I am Love, I will not hurt you; I will not let you down." I coax sweetly.

I introduce you to my friend Peace. She comes in the form of a sweet energy and brings a rushing wave of calmness to your beating heart. In an instant, your entire body relaxes.

The fear you initially felt begins to settle and then leaves altogether. Your gaze leaves mine as your body curls into a loose ball, and you allow your weight to slump against my shoulder. The burdens of today fall off of your back. The failures, rejections, and painful words you have been carrying begin to form in the pupils of your eyes as you gaze into the depth of the canyon below. I tilt your chin back to my face and meet your eyes once again. I smile as the fire dances in my eyes. "I am Love," I say gently. Peace wraps its grip around those chains of pain surrounding your heart that have held you captive. With a gentle tug, the chains fall, exposing your wounded heart. Your eyes stay locked with mine as your failures, rejections, and painful experiences begin to dissipate.

Emerged in Peace, you let your eyes wander back to the canyon. The chains you were once carrying crash to the floor of the canyon. "In my presence, chains are broken, and hearts are exposed." The voice of Love is like that of rushing water. You close your eyes to the sound of the soothing water, only to be awakened in an instance as you are being carried by a stream of peace. Your adventure has begun.

Chapter Two

My Friend Peace

Be strong and courageous. Do not fear or be in dread of them, for it is the Lord your God who goes with you. He will not leave you or forsake you. —Deuteronomy 31:6

Yarrow are gently carried to a nearby shore. You place your foot on the shore. As you begin to wring out your shirt, you take in the scenery. It is unlike anything you have ever seen. You have managed to find yourself in the center of the canyon; the sides of the canyon are glistening, and the grass is soft beneath your feet.

You gaze in front of you to find a long narrow pathway. As you take a step forward, your foot lands on something sharp. Your gaze shifts down, and you find the broken chains of your heart shattered in a million places. A smile spreads across your face, and you begin to turn in every direction looking for the one whom your soul loves. You feel the Peace still beating in your heart.

A sound similar to that of rushing water fills your ears. You begin to realize its different though; the sound turns to a feeling as that of the wind brushing up against you. To your delight, you hear a voice in the wind whisper, "Who are you looking for?" As confusion crosses your brow, you turn to see whose voice is in the wind, but it is a feeling not a being. You respond hesitantly, "I am looking for the one whom my soul desires, the one whose eyes broke the chains of my heart." The wind swirls around you. "Oh, you mean Love?" "I'm not sure," you mutter. The hum of Wind settles as the words "I am near and never far" radiate in your heart. "I don't understand," you cry out.

With a gentle and patient tone Wind responds, "Take a step of faith, my friend Peace is with you, and you must learn to trust her." The fear of the unknown begins to well up inside of you, and the "what ifs" begin to ring loudly in your ears. You gaze once again down the narrow path of the canyon, and the feeling of familiarity becomes so strong you drop to your knees and curl up in a ball among the broken chains. The hush of the stream draws your attention and then becomes deafening in your ears. You feel your heart begin to pound and your legs go numb.

The sun begins to set behind the canyon, and the cold breeze nips your ears and nose. Your mind sinks into despair, as your anxious heart cries out, "Why have you left me?" Your words echo against the canyon wall. Slowly your mind recalls the words of Wind: "My friend Peace is with you." With every ounce of faith you can muster, you call on her name, *PEACE*. Your heartbeat begins to slow; the trembling eventually coming to a halt. You stretch out your legs and place your arms under you. You slowly push yourself off the chains that once held you captive and stand to your feet.

You feel the breeze of Wind: "I am near and never far, don't stay in your brokenness, take the hand of Peace." You feel your strength renew as the beating sound of Peace entangles your newly exposed heart. She guides you down the middle of the narrowing canyon. Your eyes trace the ridges in the side of the cliffs, as your feet tread lightly into the setting sun. Your pace slows when your path narrows to a fork in the road. You come to an abrupt stop and gaze to your left and then to your right. Both directions are marked with uncharted territories weathered by the elements of nature. You have been here before, and the indecisiveness creates a familiar feeling of anxiety. After a few deep breaths, you refuse to give into your brokenness and attempt to trust Peace, even if that means doing it fearfully. She guides you to the right, and one step turns to two. Before you know it, you are gliding through an untraveled path that also continues to narrow.

The sun has left the sky, and in her place the moon shines brightly over the tops of the canyon. The crunch of the grass and rocks under your feet keep you grounded as you focus on the natural rhythm of your feet. Peace whispers to you to *take in the view*. As you look past the tops of the canyons, you see what seems to be an endless number of stars. Your breathing quickens, and you declare the letters YHWH through your inhale and exhale. You allow yourself to feel wonder and amazement; like a little child you become giddy; your heart begins to race as excitement wells within you.

Your feet begin to elevate as you suddenly realize you are rising above the canyons, above the horizon, to find yourself within the stars. The excitement rages through your body and, for the first time in your life, you realize you are completely free. You are no longer bound by the chains of the world, the limits of fear, or the expectations of man. You can feel Peace as she engulfs you with a mystery of unknown colors that dance in the sky. You begin to dance too, as your very own imagination comes alive.

You begin to leap, and man-made limitations fall from your soul. You jump a little higher, and the feeling of Love washes over you. The words "you are wanted, and you have a destiny" dance in the sky. Your heart races at these displays of affirmation, yet a small feeling of doubt crosses your mind: "Can it be true, a failure like me, wanted?" The truth of this reality becomes too much to bear; you fall to your knees as doubt overtakes your mind. Your innermost being cries out in disbelief, and you hit the ground like lightning. You find despair surrounding you in the form of chains as you cry out for Love to come. Your entire being trembles beneath the weight of despair. Peace races through your heart with comfort, but your soul cries out for the one whom you Love.

The trembling becomes too much, and the weight of fear begins to suffocate your very existence. You find yourself once again balled up in your chains. You hear a rustle in the distance and feel the weight of death, as fear has completely overtaken over your heart. The earth goes silent; the colors that once danced fade to a dark blue. Fear-stricken, you place your face to the ground. You hear footsteps coming your way, and the whole earth begins to shake. Then within the shaking, you sense a sweet presence gazing down at you. Ashamed of your failure you continue to hide your face.

You feel the warmth of His hand under your chin and the pounding in your ears stops; through trembling you look straight into the eyes of fire. You know those eyes--they are the eyes of Love. Love places His hand under your arm and guides you to your feet. He pulls you into a warm embrace as the feeling of Love engulfs you. Your fear melts away. "Be Brave." The words strike a chord, and you find yourself sobbing into the embrace of Love. "Child, perfect love casts out all fear." the words penetrate your heart as you cry out between sobs, "But I failed you! I gave into doubt. How could you ever want someone like me?" The silence lingers as you feel the Love loosen His embrace and pull away from you.

You bring your hand to your eyes and wipe the tears from your face then glance up to find Love staring at the rising sun. You find yourself still in the canyon and look around as the sun clears the morning dew. "I never wanted perfection. I just want you." You hear the emotion in His words. He turns and locks His eyes with yours, and a smile spreads across His kind, weathered face. "I am always near and never far; now march on." He says as He walks towards the rising sun.

Chapter Three

I Don't Understand Why

But, as it is written, what no eye has seen, nor ear heard, nor the heart of man imagined, what God has prepared for those who love him.
—1 Corinthians 2:9

As the faint image of Love leaves your sight, you sit and ponder His words. You feel worn and exhausted from the journey and begin to wonder what this is all for. "How did I even get here?" you cry out. Peace once again invades your partially exposed heart, as she fills you with a deep settling in your chest. You breathe in and out, once again settling your heart.

"Peace," you inquire, "what is this all for? I don't understand Love, and I don't understand why I am here and having to go through all of this." The warmth of the atmosphere shifts as you sense Peace within you processing your question. "There is a Love so great that it cannot be contained, it cannot be understood or processed within human logic; it is a Love that would crash through the universe to converse with you." The answer comes from within and burns deep within your chest. You begin to stir with anticipation, and you feel as though you have all the answers and yet none at all.

Peace begins to sense your inner struggle. The leaves rustle and the ground quakes ever so gently beneath you. Lilies begin to pop up through the canyon around you. "I want to show you something," the words well within your heart as you find yourself racing through a field of lilies. The petals blow in the wind and the colors of the lilies radiate pinks, violet, and red, shades of blues, purples, and yellows that your human mind cannot comprehend. As your running slows to a walk, you sit gently and let the lilies engulf you. The questions, worries, and desires begin to fade, and you wonder if this is eternity. With a mending heart and a quiet mind, you close your eyes and feel the cool breeze on your face as the most delightful fragrance of lavender fills your nostrils.

The sudden urge to worship overtakes you, and you are overcome with complete reverence for Love. For this entity that has completely captivated you. Tears stream down your face, and you begin to wonder what thought or question ever mattered. You are so overcome with Peace and reverence that you never want to leave. You look down at your feet and there, gracing them, are the shoes of the gospel of Peace.

You suddenly feel empowered by the comfort of knowing Peace is always within step, surrounding your heart and guiding your path. You feel the familiar breeze of Wind say, "Meet my friend Surrender." You allow your body to lay in the field of lilies, and you close your eyes. The feeling of Surrender shoots from your toes to the top of your head. In this moment with Surrender, you are overcome with gratitude, and you begin to realize the significance of the journey. You feel changed, you feel Peace, you feel Surrender.

The feeling of being wanted comes through the place of Surrender; you feel the exposed places of your heart being mended. You cry out, "I am wanted, Love wants me." As you open your eyes, the grasses dance beneath you. A newfound sense of confidence takes root in your heart. "This is what living feels like," whispers the wind.

For the first time in your life, you are exactly where you are supposed to be *for such a time as this.* With a sense of ease, you move your body to a sitting position and then you stand. You take your next step in the lily field and walk forward, leaving the baggage of the past behind. For a split second you remember those crushed chains that have followed you like a residue of memories. You watch as feelings of being unnamed and unwanted in the form of chains dissolve within your heart.

As you walk towards the setting sun, you can feel Peace around you and Surrender within you. The words, "I am always near, I am never far," ring in your ears as you hold onto your promise from the one whom your soul loves. You charge ahead aware of the growing path leading you through the valley under the treading of your feet.

Chapter Four

The Labeled Arrows

Proclaim this among the nations: Consecrate for war, stir up the mighty men. Let all the men of war draw near; let them come up. —Joel 3:9

H ow much longer?" you wonder as you pass through the never-ending valley and begin to take on the hill. As you trudge on, you become vastly aware that you have walked through the night as the rising sun pours warmth upon your face. Weariness begins to set in as you place your foot upon the diminishing hill. Peace and Surrender urge you forward as you muster the last of your strength to clear the hill and, to your surprise, you peer into a lower valley filled with wildflowers that you don't seem to recognize.

You begin to hear shouting in the distance and wonder if this is your next assignment. As you lightly run down the side of the hill and place your feet in the valley, the voices grow louder, but you can't seem to make out their shouts. Peace grows restless within you, and your heart begins to pound with the memory of Surrender. Your shoes fit tightly on your feet as you take a step towards the shouts.

The clouds begin to form around the sun, the grass in the valley begins to sway, and the sky darkens. Wind starts to whip the side of your face as it whispers, "run." Your feet begin to carry you through the valley past the wildflowers, away from the safety of the valley and straight into a war zone. You come to an abrupt halt as the horrific war scene takes your breath away. Thunder begins to roll through the clouds as rain and flashes of lightning touch the ground. You see bodies of warriors on every inch of land as arrows fly through the air.

A crash of thunder shakes the earth as you lose your balance and fall to the ground. Shouting grows loud in your ears, and you begin to lose your sense of hearing. Your head begins to pound along with heavy rainfall that causes your ears to ring and your body to shake as you become disoriented. Your eyes flutter open as you stare straight into a small puddle forming. Your nose drips droplets of water, as you consciously try to slow your breathing. The shouts turn to screeches as you slowly pull yourself off the ground. With wobbly legs, you lift your head and see wounded warriors lying as far as your eyes can see. Thunder crashes again shaking your senses once more. You look to your right and glance down at a wounded man, pale and trembling. His eyes lock with yours and the darkness within them makes you shudder.

Your gaze rests on his chest, and you are overcome with confusion as hundreds of arrows take form around his heart. His breathing grows shallow as his eyes search your face. The rain clouds your vision as a mixture of blood and water flood the tops of your shoes. Shouts grow in the distance. Your eyes catch a glimpse of a warrior standing a few yards from you, his sopping dark hair nestled into the nape of his neck, his shoulders broad, and his eyes dark. Your gaze catches his lips as a venomous arrow leaves his mouth striking a woman across from him. The arrow drives straight into the woman's heart. She regards the man for a moment until her legs give out from under her and she slips to the ground. Another crack of thunder startles you to your senses as your mind races with the thought, "I have to get out of here." You slip to your knees as you watch the woman struggle to breathe as she clutches the arrow secure in her heart.

You lift your head again to see the same dark-haired man standing over the woman as several arrows fly from his mouth straight into her weakening heart. You begin to cry out "NO," but the words will not release from your lips. You try again as you are overcome with terror, and only soft, broken syllables leave your mouth echoing the patter of the rain. Through the downpour, your eyes catch a glimpse of the dark-haired man now joined by many others. You watch as venomous arrow after arrow flies from their mouths and hits standing and wounded warriors alike. You watch as arrows drive into the depth of hearts, minds, and souls.

A hellish feeling overtakes you as you hit your hands on the ground and grasp at loose mud. Terror and rage overtake you as you scream, "AHHHHH!" You lift your head to the sky and watch as it grows darker to the point of complete occlusion. You watch as fires rage in the east and volcanoes erupt in the west. Men and women alike spew arrows at wounded warriors as though in competition with one another, taking pride in the screams of the wounded.

You see arrows consuming some warriors to the point where they are not even recognizable. Your attention is pulled from the scene as a man trips and stumbles right in front of you. Fear-stricken but curious, your eyes wander to his trembling face and see an arrow wedged in his temple. Stunned, you reach your hand out and trace the words "Pastor" above the fletching of the arrow. Your gaze shifts to his heart where you find another arrow wedged deep with the word "Father." As your fingers brush the word he screams in terror. You rip your hand from the arrow and watch as the corner of his mouth drips with blood.

Thunder crashes and you lunge back on your heels; your hands begin to sweat as you feel a sudden urge to remove the arrow from the wounded warrior. You once again crawl on all fours towards the warrior, his face lined with agony. As you inch forward, you are overcome with the smell of the festering wound and hold your breath to prevent vomiting. As you reach for the arrow in his chest and rest your fingers on the fletching, you give it a firm tug. The warrior screams out and sits straight up, looks you right in the eyes and screams, "What are you doing? Don't take my idol, I need that."

Fear grips your heart as you jump back and release the arrow. "Get me out of here," you scream. Despair fills your soul as you sob and fold under the pressure of the chaos around you. You fall face first into the mud as the stench fills your lungs; your breathing grows shallow. Your sobbing becomes so heavy it begins to drown out the screeching. The darkness clouds your vision; thunder rolls and lightning strikes; your body goes numb as the rain forces you to close your eyes. "Love, save me," you whisper with one last ray of hope. Suddenly, the earth goes silent. Rain droplets fall from your nose and tap the ground. You open your eyes to see yourself surrounded by grass in a green valley. Trembling and confused you whisper, "Love, where are you?" "I am here," Love responds.

Chapter Five

Love is a Person

See what kind of love the Father has given to us,
that we should be called children of God; and so
we are. The reason why the world does not know
us is that it did not know him. —1 John 3:1

You feel the presence of Love as you lift yourself off the ground and back to a sitting position directly across from Love. You are overcome with gratitude and thankful you are away from the battlefield--and then the anger sets in. "How could you put me through that?" you scream at Love. But Love remains quiet as He looks into the distance. Your eyes trace His sharp features yet gentle gaze. You let your eyes roam to the most magnificent rainbow you have ever laid eyes on.

You gasp as if the beauty is too much to behold. You feel Peace come over you and tears drop from your eyes and grow warm on your cheeks. You feel a hand lightly grasp yours and you grasp His without moving your gaze from the colors dancing in the sky. The air is calm; Peace is in the stillness and questions begin to race through your head once again. You hold your tongue and, with your hand still in Love's, you keep your eyes intently on the rainbow. The colors dance on the beams. They change from bright to radiant to majestic; you watch as the rainbow changes colors before your eyes. Love brushes next to you, and you instinctively rest your head on his shoulder and the familiar memories of your time with Him on top of the canyon fill your mind. The feeling of His strong shoulder and soft hand brings you great comfort.

You breathe in one last breath as you pull your gaze from the rainbow and up to Love's face. His gaze meets yours and, to your surprise, you see the rainbow dancing in His eyes. The majestic colors dance around His pupils in such a radiant way. As your gaze moves from his eyes to his cheeks you see they are tear stained. You continue to gaze down until your eyes fall on his lips. His graceful lip line begins to move as you hear, "My children are so broken and hurting."

Moved to tears by Love's response, you meet his eyes once again and see those familiar fire-filled eyes. Words refuse to leave your lips, as you stare deeper into His eyes. The entire world begins to flash through them as war scenes and brokenness tell a story of the ages. You are overcome with such humility and reverence that you bow your head and begin to sense the glory you are sitting in. Love reaches out His hand and picks up your chin. He slowly moves towards you and lightly brushes His lips on your forehead as if He knows your very thoughts and feelings.

You wrap your arms around him in a deep embrace. For the first time in your entire life, you have been seen, you have been heard, and yet nothing was said. You return to your position sitting next to Him in the lush of the grass. Your hand once again finds His as you rest your head against His shoulder. "Child," He says as His gaze stays on the rainbow, "what you saw today was the spirit of hate running rampant in the world. Where there is no Love, my children turn inward." Shocked by His words, the questions begin to form in your mind. You move your head from His shoulder and turn your body to face Him; you wrap your arms around your legs, and He nods in approval.

"I saw an angry man with venomous arrows coming out of his mouth and the arrow struck a woman," you stutter in broken words, "and the stench, and sounds, and the arrows with labels, it was all too much an..and I was afraid." Your body quakes with the details of the memories. Love turns His gaze to you as you watch the familiar scenes play out once again in the eyes of Love. A tear falls from His eye. He turns and stares back at the rainbow and says, "The rainbow you see is a covenant I made with man, but yet I am still rejected.

"Lies and deceit cause man to stumble. What you saw today was my children spewing words of hurt and rejection upon those I instructed them to love. You also saw burrowed arrows of manmade identities that turn to idols and, in turn, wound those I love. Those who are wounded hold tightly to the arrows within their hearts, terrified that they will be ripped from them."

You stare in disbelief as you begin to investigate your own heart, wondering what arrows have been shot at you throughout the years. "Does every arrow that hits its target have to stay?" you sputter anxiously. Love gazes knowingly into your heart. "No, my child, only the ones you make idols of and choose to keep-- it's your choice, it always has been yours. You see many arrows are shot by self-righteous people. Those who are wounded hold on to the arrow as self-preservation and, oftentimes, make idols out of the accusations as a way to prove their accusers wrong. Those arrows can get wedged into hearts for years and then they become almost impossible to see. I ask my children to turn over their idols and words of rejection to me, but they feel as though they are losing their identity when in reality, they have lost their life."

You move your gaze from Love and notice the rainbow has been replaced with a dark sky. Without removing your gaze from the darkness, you ask Love with a shaky voice, "If the arrows become a part of us, then how do we remove them from our heart?" Love responds knowingly, "The arrow can only be removed when you let me become a part of your heart. You see child, it is out of relationship with me that you realize there is an arrow, and out of that relationship you have chosen to realize the arrow was never yours to carry. Lastly, out of that relationship you find value and realize the name of the arrow and are given the strength to remove it from your midst. You see child, you need me--Love."

The words ring true in your ears as you muster one last glance into His eyes of fire. He looks at you knowingly. "The man you saw today, he is one of my sons, a Pastor and a Father. He was rejected by his congregation, which struck his mind, and later by his son, which struck his heart. He made an idol out of his pain and then an identity out of his rejection. My child, only I can remove the arrow from his mind and heart, but he must come to me." Before you can even ask "how?" He responds, "Relationship child, relationship is sought by you. When you stay on the journey, and keep your eyes locked with mine, then it is possible."

He reaches out his hand and strokes your cheek. He then stands and begins to walk away from you. Your heart leaps as you yell out after him, "Where are you going?" Love turns and with a kind smile and shouts back, "I am always near and never far."

You brush your own cheek where His fingers rested just seconds before and watch as He slips into the night sky. You burrow into the grass beneath you and close your eyes. You feel your body slip into a deep sleep as you are comforted by the words of Love.

Chapter Six

The Cactus

It was I who knew you in the wilderness, in the land of drought; —Hosea 13:5

The heat of the sun blazing on your face awakens you from your slumber. You place your hands next to you and suddenly feel the grit of sand. Confused, you open your eyes and brush the sand from your hands only to find yourself surrounded by desert. Your mouth is dry and your body stiff. You begin to take in the view of the sand as mounds of it blows gracefully across the desert. You scan the horizon and find nothing but miles and miles of sand; not a cloud in the sky just the sun blaring in your eyes with intense strength. "I went to bed in a green valley and awoke in the desert, how can this be?" You think this to yourself as you push yourself to your feet and lightly nudge something in the process. You look down to see a backpack with a note attached to the front.

You kneel down and allow your fingers to trace the note as you tear it off and read, "Dear Child, you will need this on the journey set before you." You have become familiar with the unpredictability of Love, but your trust in who He is has grown. You place the note in your pocket and reach down and pull at the zipper. It will not budge. You try again with some grit, but the zipper is stuck. With a sigh of defeat, you pick up the backpack and place it on your back. As the sun rises high in the sky, you pick a direction based on your gut instinct and begin to walk. The journey starts out easy as you cover miles of sand.

You begin to make out a shadow in the distance and your heart begins to pound, unsure of what you are about to approach. You bring your hand up to shield your eyes. You squint and, after a few seconds, you make out the form of what looks like a cactus. You begin to walk towards it. As you approach the cactus, you make out its height and long spikes then determine it is best to continue walking as far away from it as you can get. As you continue on, your eyes spot a tree. Desperate for some shade, you sprint lightly to the tree. You struggle with the sand under your shoes and desperation in your soul. You approach what looks to be an Acacia Tree, but the closer you get to it the further the tree gets. Frustrated, you consider the possibility that the tree is a mirage, and so you walk in the opposite direction.

As defeat kicks in and the desire for some shade from the sun sets your heart on that goal, you sit in the middle of the desert and drop your backpack at your side. You place your hands at your side and feel something soft brush against your fingertips. Your hand touches the most beautiful yet delicate plant you have ever seen. You brush a petal of the plant lightly; the wind gently blows across your face; you recognize the plant to be a Living Stone. You place your hand at the base of the plant and give it a tug and watch as it disappears within your grasp. You look for the plant desperately in all directions and find only sand.

You gaze in the direction of the sun to see it still firmly in place, as if time has stopped. Your mind begins to race and, unsure of where to go, you stand and walk. Once again you are drawn to the shadow of the cactus, the mirage of the Acacia Tree and, lastly, the smooth feeling of the Living Stone Plant as you plop down in the sand out of frustration. You close your eyes and envision each item as it caught your attention: the spikes on the cactus, the shade of the tree, and the feeling of the Living Stone Plant. The desert sun grows warm on your face, and the backpack feels heavy on your back. You let it fall at your side and rest your head on the front of the backpack. Exhaustion sets deep in your bones as the sand lightly settles in the cracks of your skin.

You feel like crying but tears will not come. You sit up and gaze in the distance where you see a nearby sand mound. "Maybe it's just a mirage?" your mind questions, but it is the first thing that has looked remotely different than the miles of sand you have walked. So, you lift your body from the sand, pick up your backpack and walk towards it. As you approach the mound, your heart grows frustrated with the journey and the heavy sand under your feet. You approach the bottom of the mound and begin to climb it, but with each step, you slide a few feet down. The more you climb the deeper you slide. Your heart wrenches as you fall to your knees and the sand surrounds you.

The desert sun has nearly consumed your energy, and you are growing wearier by the moment. As you look to the right of the mound, you see that same familiar shadow of a cactus. With great sense of defeat, you slump over. "How did I get here and where do I go?" you scream out. The familiar voice of Wind whispers, "Keep going and use what you have been given." Instantly you remember the backpack. You remove it from your back once again and place your fingers on the zipper. With a great tug you unzip the backpack and this time it opens with ease. You squeal with delight and reach inside. Your fingers brush something metal, and you pull out a compass. You allow it to rest in the palm of your hand as you analyze the gold casing and study its face.

This compass is unlike any you have ever seen. Instead of directions, the magnetic needle points to a cactus. You look down at the backpack with great wonder only to find it zipped back in place. You know better than to try to unzip it. So, you return it to your back, wipe the dust from your brow, stand up and march towards the shadow of the cactus. As you approach the cactus you notice its immense height and long spines. You don't dare go too close for fear it will once again penetrate your heart.

You allow yourself to sit a good distance away and bring your gaze up from the base of the cactus to the top. With admiration in your eyes, you begin to examine the cactus. You analyze the details of its spines, height, color, and depth. The wind begins to blow with a strong consistency. The sand swirls, and you become engulfed in it as you lose sight of the cactus. The sand grows so strong that it cakes heavy in your mouth, ears, and eyes. You place your head down as it pelts you from all directions. The heavy whistle of the wind brings confusion to your mind.

The sand is so strong you cannot speak out loud. Instead within your heart you ask for help. A familiar feeling of Surrender embraces your thoughts, as memories of emotional sandstorms fill your mind. You begin to wonder if you are slipping from consciousness. The wind grows stronger, and your body begins to slip into darkness as the memories and visions of hurt and pain dance in your mind-- memories of betrayal, loss, and rejection play like a musical in your ears. You can see, smell, and even touch the very places of pain you have walked through, as if a movie of your life is on display for all to see.

The pain of the scene becomes so intense it is as if you are living all of your trauma all over again. You wish to die; your physical body cracks under the pressure of the sandstorm as you fall to your face. The sand whips your skin violently, and you are brought back to the senses of your current circumstance. You grasp onto floating sand as it rips through your fingers. You feel your entire body being blown in different directions as you attempt to hold onto anything that might save you. It becomes evident that your own strength will not save you, so within your spirit you allow Surrender to continue invading your heart.

During the storm, Peace washes over you, and you begin to give life to the memories of pain. You allow yourself to Surrender to the memories displayed in the sand as they blow violently around you and within you. The biting and whipping pain of the memories begin to feel like an eternal windstorm happening around you, as you are being depleted of what you have held onto for all these years. You begin to cry out within the sand as memories and pain blow into the storm, until the violent winds rest. Trembling and shaking, you cautiously open your eyes to see the sand is now still and the grandness of the cactus is before you.

Completely empty, you push yourself to your knees and begin to sob from the tenderness of Surrender. "You are the cactus," the words come from the cactus itself. You gaze deeply at it as the spikes continue to vibrate. "Your outer stature has become a cactus to those you encounter; people fear getting too close to you. You assume that the spines of your exterior keep the pain away, but you have not accounted for the fact that they also keep Love out. You are dry and alone, with a hard exterior." The spines of the cactus begin to shrivel as the words are spoken. "You became the cactus through the pains of this world, and each spine grew longer and stronger as you created a version of yourself through your own strength as a way to protect what was on the inside. Only through Surrender, as you cast your cares to the sand, will the cactus dissolve."

The spines of the cactus fold within itself and turn to dust, just as the last words ring in your ears. You crumble under the weight of pain and allow yourself to let go. You watch as the painful memories sweep up into the gentleness of the wind, as they blow around you and then behind you. You raise your hands in the air as the remainder of your pain and rejection leaves your body. A glimmer of light shines in the darkness of your heart and casts a light that you can see in the exterior of your chest. You lift your eyes to the desert, completely depleted but finally alive.

Chapter Seven

The Acacia Tree

By which He has granted to us His precious and very great promises, so that through them you may become partakers of the divine nature, having escaped from the corruption that is in the world because of sinful desire. —2 Peter 1:4

Desperate for your thirst to be quenched, you lift your weary body up and begin to walk in the desert as the sand whips lightly around you. You are completely empty from the memories of pain that you gave to the sand. You feel as though nothing can hold you back, but also as though there is no incentive to propel you forward. Unsure of where to go next, you find your compass tapping your thigh within the rhythm of your stride. You place your hand in your pocket and pull it out. The magnetic needle points to the shadow of a small tree.

The shadow of the tree is nowhere in sight, but you follow the arrow towards the setting sun. The desert begins to feel cool as the sun slips behind the clouds, and you welcome a much-needed breeze. Sand etches throughout every pore of your body. You are dirty, empty, and depleted, but you sense Peace and Surrender are with you.

There is sand as far as your eyes can see. It looks like an eternal blanket resting on the wholeness of creation. You squint your eyes as a large shadow begins to form in the distance. A feeling of hope begins to take root in your heart, and you run towards the familiar shadow aware of the mirage of the shade you once encountered. The faster you run, the closer the shadow appears. Soon you can see the outline of the tree, and this time it is real.

Panic races through your body as the settling sun glistens off the shadow of the distant tree. You trudge towards the tree mustering the last of your adrenaline. The tree is no longer a shadow. You come to an abrupt stop and stare at the tree with intensity. Panic and anxiety settle throughout your body, and your heart races so fast you are convinced it may burst through your chest. Thoughts in your once empty mind begin to swirl. "The journey has been so long that I can't bear another obstacle, or worse, a mirage of false hope."

The thoughts continue to talk to you as though a mysterious, inner source is spewing lies to your own mind. "What if the tree brings memories of pain and rejection? What if I feel the pain of loss in my core as if I am living it all over again? What if it will beat me down as my body endures more physical pain? I don't think I can take any more." The thoughts themselves become unbearable, as your legs tremble beneath you. The sun continues to slip behind the horizon and the sands are still. In an effort to turn off your mind, you stare into the distance at the standing tree—waiting for an answer.

You stand for what seems like hours. The sun has disappeared, and you are surrounded by a cloud of darkness. Yet you are unable to move. You are completely frozen by the fear of "what if." With your legs still trembling beneath you, you swallow hard as the desire for water grows strong. You gaze down at the compass still in your hand as it points to the tree. You must decide, or the indecisiveness will kill you. You loosen your shoulders and allow your backpack to fall to the ground. You kneel down hoping for an answer. Your fingers find the zipper and you give a tug. Again, and to your dismay, it will not budge.

In a state of numbness, you distinctively place your backpack in its rightful place, stand, and stare onward. The stars begin to fill the night sky making the desert sand glow with light. Your eyes stay fixed on the tree. You take one shaky step towards it. Wind begins to blow, with the words "onward my child". You place one foot in front of the other as panic and anxiety fill you, still you move. Each shaky step becomes heavy under the weight of fear—still you move.

Your body aches from the journey, and your heart begs you to stop and rest, but still you move. Your shaky strides quicken until you can smell the tree. The fragrance fills your nostrils with a strong sense of honey, a refreshing smell that washes over you as you melt into its sweet aroma. You lift your gaze to a view of its strong branches and delicate leaves. Your hand follows the sturdy bark until it rests at the base of the tree, and you allow your body to lower and sit.

Your gaze takes in every detail of the tree's magnificent stature. The leaves are in full bloom, bright and glistening, and the smell of honey begins to overpower you as you slowly curl up against the stump of the tree. Overcome by gratitude, you rest your sore bones. Within the shelter of the tree your fear and trembling stop. Peace, your kindred friend, washes over your depleted soul. Your weary back gives way to your backpack as it slips to your side. Your eyes glance down and notice the backpack is unzipped. You reach in and pull out a canteen of water.

Tears of thanksgiving fill your eyes as you bring the canteen to your cracked lips and allow the richness of cool water to quench your dry throat. The substance gives strength to your bones. Your eyes become heavy under the renewal of the richness you smell and the water you taste. Your eyes flutter with heaviness as you desperately try to stay awake. "Sleep under the shelter of the Acacia Tree as your soul is renewed." These words from Wind surround you like a blanket of Peace as the heaviness overtakes your eyes. "Rest Child."

Chapter Eight

His Blood is Enough

In him we have redemption through his blood, the forgiveness of our trespasses, according to the riches of his grace, which he lavished upon us, in all wisdom and insight. **—Ephesians 1:7-8**

The sun dances against your closed eyes, as you sense your body awaken from a deep slumber. You open one eye and then the other, taking in the bright sun shining all around. You look up to see the Acacia Tree providing just enough shade to shield your eyes from the direct glare of the sun. Your body is calm and rested. For the first time in a while, you feel completely calm.

You look to your right and see your zipped backpack. You stretch out your legs and look down to see your shoes of the gospel of Peace and instantly remember the beauty of meeting Surrender. Your eyes move to the ground around you and see a simple yellow flower. You recognize it as a Golden Sun Cup; then as far as you can see there are perfect yellow flowers with an infused red center. You gaze upon the multitudes of Golden Sun Cups and are overcome with the delicate way they blow in the wind.

Each flower is unique to its maker as they sit on top of the sand unplanted and subject to the breeze.

Footsteps draw your focus away from the flowers as the sound approaches and your heart races. The steps grow louder as you grow more anxious and wrap your arms tightly around your chest. Your eyes look around desperately searching for someone, but no one is around.

You raise your eyes to the top of the trees and see the leaves begin to rustle. Your mouth fills with moisture and the air grows heavy; you sense rain forming in the clouds. The once hot desert sun begins to disappear behind rain clouds, and the sky grows dark. The steps come to an abrupt stop. A few steps from where you sit stands a stoic figure. His face is calm, his cheekbones high, and his lips are held tightly in a thin line. His stature is strong and tall, and his eyes are blue like the ocean. Your body lunges hard against the base of the tree. Your hands grasp for security as you push them into the ground next to you, and your eyes meet with those of the stoic figure. You mutter, "Wh...who are you?" His eyes seem to stare straight into your soul. Your gaze leaves his and catches the Golden Sun Cups as they begin to blow in the wind. Your legs shake as you wrap your hands securely around them once again to stop the trembling.

The wind stirs as the dark clouds shift across the sky. You bring your eyes back to the stoic figure. His entire body is covered in a red cloak. He holds a large sword that he grasps with confidence. Your heart leaps with fear; you begin to panic but you are too weak to move. He senses you staring at the sword and gracefully moves it in the air. Reflexively, you lunge back again, but your eye catches something inscribed in the blade of the sword. You squint your eyes and read the inscription: "The Blood is Enough." Your eyes widen in amazement as you muster the courage to meet his ocean blue eyes. His eyes soften as he says with authority, "I am Redemption."

His words sear like fire, and the earth seems to weep as rain soaks the desert and lightning strikes creating a geological phenomenon. The shafts of light mimic the path of the lightning bolt as it disperses into the ground. Thunder crashes loudly in the distance and startles you, so that you jump to your feet. Redemption stands firm and unmoved by the lightning and thunder. You wrap your arms around your chest and huddle closer to the Acacia Tree trying to stay dry.

The wind continues to blow as your body spasms with each crack of thunder. Redemption meets your eyes and His face shines brightly allowing your body to calm. He moves the sword in his hand and points down with the blade to the last remaining Golden Sun Cup. Still holding onto the tree, you slowly reach out and grab it. Once in your hand you examine it. The perfect shade of yellow covers every petal, and in the center are perfect drops of red encasing the pistil. "The blood is enough" --the words echo loudly as Redemption firmly speaks within a crash of thunder.

Rain falls from the branches of the tree in heavy drops soaks the Golden Sun Cup in your hand until it crumbles. Water drips off of your eyelashes onto your nose and down your chin as your gaze moves from the flower to Redemption. You feel your strength being renewed as you ask, "What are you trying to show me?" You grow bolder and demand an answer from Redemption. A smile spreads across Redemption's face "the blood is enough; it covers your sin; it's your strength and it's your renewal. It replaces the emptiness and brings substance to your depleted, empty shell."

The depth of Redemption's words impacts your depleted soul as you fall to your knees accompanied by the strike of a lightning bolt. You feel the weight of power in the blood. You hear the footsteps of Redemption turn from you and walk into the storm. The lightning once again strikes and thunder crashes. You welcome Surrender to come as you let go of yourself, your wants, and your desires. "You are righteous." This thought forms involuntarily within you.

A feeling of renewal begins to form in your soul, invades your mind, and bursts to the tips of your fingers and toes. You hear the rain begin to slow to a simple pitter patter rhythm. The leaves drip small droplets of water onto your head, and you feel a cleansing begin where there was once a void. The place of emptiness you once felt disappears as you are filled with the revelation of the power in the blood.

You raise your head and to your amazement, you see Love in the distance. With a lightness in your heart, you stand and run to Him. The light rhythm of the rain comes as a cool welcome as it rolls off your face. You reach Love; you see those familiar eyes of fire smiling at you. You throw your arms around His neck. He embraces you, He lifts your chin and looks deep into your eyes, "The blood was shed for you, and it is enough." Tears sting your face as Love releases you and kneels in the sand. He picks up a Golden Sun Cup. He looks up at you, and you instinctively kneel next to Him. He moves His hand gently to your face and places the Golden Sun Cup behind your ear. "The renewal has begun." The words He speaks sound so gentle and sweet.

You bring your hand to the flower behind your ear and gently stroke the petals as your gaze remains locked with Love. Love reaches down again and picks another Golden Sun Cup from the damp ground. He places the flower into your palm, as your eyes trace the perfect yellow bloom. The deep red in the center catches your attention. "Redemption is nothing without the blood, but like this flower they are a part of each other. The color cannot be separated. With the blood comes redemption and with redemption comes the blood. The gift of redemptive blood is yours." You bring the flower to your chest and press it against your heart.

You stare down at the Golden Sun Cups surrounding you as tears fall from your eyes. The flower pressed against your chest takes the form of a gold breastplate with a perfect red center. You place your hand on the breastplate astonished by the power and beauty of it. Your eyes filled with questions find Love's. He lets out a laugh. "That is the breastplate of Righteousness. It confirms that you are now right-standing with me, and nothing can separate you and me. That, my child, is the redemptive power of the blood." Overcome with questions, you can only form one thought. "What blood?" "Ahhh," Love responds, "the blood of my Son. You will meet Him soon, and He will call you *chosen*." Your eyes widen as you are overcome with a knowing of your rightful place on this journey.

The sun begins to poke through the clouds. You turn your face to its warmth and close your eyes, letting the heat rest on your face as the renewal brings life to the dry places in your heart. You turn your face back to Love and find that He is gone. You stand and walk towards the Acacia Tree but notice it has also vanished. You walk the distance reclaiming the ground back to your backpack. You kneel, pick it up and place it on your back. You pull your compass out of your pocket and notice the magnetic needle pointing to the Living Stone Plants. With your shoes on and breastplate in place, you walk in the direction of the magnetic needle.

Chapter Nine

Lion of Judah

And one of the elders said to me, "Weep no more; behold, the Lion of the tribe of Judah, the Root of David, has conquered, so that he can open the scroll and its seven seals. —Revelation 5:5

The sun grows high in the sky marking midday, as you trudge forward following the magnetic needle that points to the image of the Living Stone Plants. With only sand in sight, you trust the compass as you put one foot in front of the other for what feels like hours.

Nightfall casts a dark glow over the sand and, weary from your travels, you decide to huddle down for the night. You drop your backpack in the sand and brace your body against it for warmth as you shiver under the cold dark sky. Hunger and thirst grip at you as you rock back and forth keeping your mind on the rhythm of the motion. You become discouraged as hunger pains growl; thoughts of discouragement become disheartening. "I thought I overcame these feelings of defeat during my journey of renewal, and here they are pressing in once again." Doubts continue to spiral. In an effort to stop the thoughts, you lift your head and glance at the closed zipper on your backpack.

But you do not even bother to try and unzip it. You fall into a restless slumber.

You awaken to a gentle breeze and allow your eyes to adjust to the brightness of the rising sun. You sit up and brush the sand off your clothing. It seems that every inch of you is coated, and you give into frustration and stop. You stand and continue to walk again not even glancing at your compass.

The desert is still. Your head spins with thoughts of the past. Your accomplishments make you proud and your failures make you shudder. "What is the point of this journey anyway?" You say these words out loud. The desert sand blows around you lightly, and you pause waiting for a nudge from Wind. But all that meets you is eerie silence. The loneliness wraps itself around your mind now full of doubts. "I thought you said you were always near and never far?" You yell out, hoping Love will appear and still nothing. The stillness begins to settle deep into your soul as you grasp for some type of feeling. "Love, Peace, Redemption--are you there?" Nothing.

You begin to pound your breastplate to bring feeling back to your flesh, your mind spinning in circles as you desperately try to feel. You find yourself crying out for any feeling at all. "Fear, anxiety, doubt? Are you there?" Nothing. You feel nothing. You frantically reach into your pocket, pull out your compass, and gaze upon the magnetic needle that still points to the image of Living Stone Plants. The numbness rings loud in your ears with nothing but sand in sight. Your thoughts become empty, your actions motionless, and your soul becomes so out of touch with reality that you are unaware of your feet moving beneath you.

Sunsets and sunrises come and go. You have no idea how long you have been walking in the fog of a desert. You have no idea how many days have passed with this heavy numbness clouding your judgement. "This must be how the journey ends." The thought jerks your attention back to reality, and you slowly let your knees hit the sand. You bring your hand to your face as you outline the cracks in your skin. You lick your dry and bleeding lips; you bring your hand to your stomach. "When is the last time you even growled?"

The thought comes and goes as past memories flash, colored with failures and victories to reflect upon. As your mind scrambles to focus on the future, you are met with a dark hole. Your hands fall at your sides, and your eyes search for some kind of hope in the distance, but you are met with miles and miles of sand. Your body aches under the feeling of defeat. Then you finally feel something. The feeling deep within forces you to fall face down into the sand. Your eyes shut tightly as the sand covers every inch of your body as it sinks deeper. You feel your body slipping into the darkness you had gazed into moments before. With a feeling of utter defeat, you let your body go.

The heat of the sand burns your skin. But as you slip deeper, the cool effect of the depth you slip into begin to touch the darkness in your mind; your breathing begins to lessen; your senses hibernate. You take one last deep breath and slip into the darkness. Within the darkness appears a small light. You gaze at it longingly and watch as the form of a hand appears and stretches towards you. You are unable to feel or move within the darkness. You watch as the light begins to disperse until all that is left is darkness--empty darkness. "When light is absent there is only darkness left." The words came from the belly of the darkness. "In the darkness nothing is felt." The words roared out of the belly with a haunting laughter. A deep sob can be heard, and you recognize it as your own. In the distance you once again catch a small glimmer of light.

You then feel your body being carried from the cool of the earth back through the heat of the sand. Suddenly your eyes jerk open as you see a hand on your breastplate pulling you up to your feet. You cough and sputter while sand spews out of your mouth. You bring your hand to your face and wipe the remaining sand out of your eyes. You regain full vision and yet see no one around. Confusion of what is real and what is not makes your head spin. You feel the familiar breeze of Wind as the words, "What are you doing?" ring in your ears. Tears begin to flow as your senses and thoughts return to your body. "I... I don't know," you sob out, "I'm so tired. I have been in this desert for so long, I don't know where to go, an..and I just want to be done." The tears turn to sobs as your body shakes under the weight of your despair.

The feelings and emotions come with a blow of loneliness. "You don't get to give up," Wind argues rather insensitively. "Did you not hear me?" you yell back. "I am done. I don't know what kind of game this is, but it hurts, it's too hard, and I AM DONE." Wind is still, and for once you are grateful. You sink back into the sand, desperate to find an ounce of Peace. "Where is your backpack?" Wind asks cautiously. "What an odd question" you think. "I don't know, and I don't care," you stutter under your breath.

The feeling of desperation sets in as you jump to your feet and begin frantically looking for it. "How could I have left it? It was my only source of hope." Your thoughts run wild as you retrace your steps, turning left and right, looking in front of you and then behind you, but all you see is sand. The air grows heavy as you sense nightfall descending once again, claiming the sky. The desperation grows so heavy that you shout out, "Wind, help me find it! That was my only hope to finish this journey." Wind is still. You sink to your knees, the exhaustion of the journey setting in without an ounce of hope. "Walk," Wind whispers. "What? Are you crazy?" you yell back. "Can't you see I'm exhausted? Can't you see I'm weary? Can't you see I have nothing left?" Wind is still.

With an angry heart, and a last bit of strength, you stand. You place your right foot out in front of you and then your left, your eyes downcast upon the familiar view of your shoes still on your feet, and a small sense of Peace returns. You walk ever so slowly as you bring your hand to your chest to feel your heart beating heavily under the armor of your breastplate, a sense of belonging and righteousness fill your mind. With each step forward you feel your hope being restored. "LOOK!" The voice of Wind startles you from your thoughts and you jerk your head up. Your eyes meet a small figure in the distance. You squint to see what it is and make out the familiar straps of your backpack. A sense of urgency fills your heart, and you quicken your pace as a surge of energy propels you forward.

As you reach the old, worn backpack, you kneel beside it, place your hand on the zipper and give it a tug, but it doesn't budge. Your heart grows heavy with discouragement as you tug a little harder--but nothing. The sting of tears fills your eyes, and you bring your hand to your weary face and aggressively wipe them away before they can fall. "Why are you doing this to me?" you cry out. "Try again," Wind urges. You grasp your fingers around the zipper and give it another tug and it opens just slightly at the seam. "Keep going," says Wind. Inch by inch the zipper opens. Relief washes over you as you place your hand in the bag. You feel a wood block and you pull it out. You stare down at the block of wood placed firmly in the palm of your hand. Your eyes trace the face of a lion.

Tearfully euphoric, a deep sense of contentment washes over you. You become overwhelmed with a feeling of happiness as tears stream down your face. You bring the wood lion close to your face and stare into its eyes. There is a certain familiarity as the eyes pierce your soul, and the cool breeze blows around you as you finally recognize the fire placed deeply in the pupils. The eyes that changed your life stare brightly back at you.

A shriek of laughter rises in your belly and roars out of your mouth. Overcome with laughter, you listen as it fills the desert air. The mouth of the lion carved so neatly on the wood block moves ever so lightly as you hear the words "joy is your strength." A purple powder leaks from the lion's mouth and spills into your hand; it emits a fragrance of lavender. Your tears drip into the eyes of the lion and the block vanishes from your hand. You gaze at the residue of power left in its place and bring the sweet-smelling aroma to your nose. You breathe it in; you feel your skin heal from the desert wind and your cracked lips fill with moisture. The corner of your eye catches a color in the distance and a form takes shape. There are plants in the distance, and their vibrance pierces your eyes. "Living Stone Plants," Wind yells. You leap in the air and race towards the Living Stone Plants.

Chapter Ten

The Keys

I will give you the keys of the kingdom of heaven;
whatever you bind on earth will be bound in heaven,
and whatever you loose on earth will be loosed in
heaven. —**Matthew 16:19**

"The time is now." The words of Wind leap in your
heart as you run towards the Living Stone Plants.
"Perhaps this is the moment I was created for." This
thought propels you forward as you reach the delicate
plants. You brace for impact as you approach the
plants. Your run slows to a walk and then you stop.
You stare at the vibrant shades of the plants before
you. The plants are clustered tightly together, each
unique in design, shape, and color. You reach forward
to touch the plants, but you are suddenly blocked by a
large piece of wood. Unaware of what is happening,
you take a step back.

To your amazement you see a large wooden door
placed directly in your line of sight. The door is
directly between you and the plants. As you move to
your right, the door moves with you, and the same
happens when you move to your left. There is no way
around the door: you must go through it. You take a
few steps towards the door and reach your hand out
to grab the knob. You turn it only to realize it is locked.

"Well surely there's a key. I must get to the plants," you think aloud. You remove your backpack and notice it is zipped. You give a tug anyway and, to your delight, the backpack unzips with ease. You reach inside and pull out a parchment scroll with the delicately traced words, "Love has the key."

You take in every inch of the scroll looking for further instructions, but nothing is there. You turn the scroll over and still nothing. You roll the scroll back in place and tuck it away in your backpack for safe keeping and return the backpack to its rightful place. You turn from the door and examine the desert behind you. "You are always near and never far," you say under your breath. The wind begins to blow. The sky turns from shades of pink and purple to orange and red. Fascinated by the changing colors, you gaze intently at the sky. The sand dances gracefully around you as joy wells up inside you. Your heart skips a beat. "He's coming," shouts Wind.

Deep anticipation grows in your heart. You hear a melody in the distance with shouts of "He's coming, He's coming, Love is coming!" The colors form to the beat of the music; the wind picks up the sand and gently turns it from right to left within the rhythm of the melody. The clouds' part and the sun forms gold shards of brilliance within the sand. You turn as the one your heart loves step out from the cloud. His eyes of fire pierce yours as He walks towards you. Your body goes numb, and you instantly fall to your knees.

A feeling of reverence overcomes you as the heavy presence of Love shakes the earth.

The presence of your Creator feels like a rushing waterfall as the power and beauty mix. Your mind begins to replay every moment of the journey, the good and the bad, the beautiful things you saw, and the hard moments you experienced as well. You suddenly realize Love was a part of every single moment. All this time, you were step-in-step with Love, and yet you were unaware of who He is. In your darkest moments He was there with an encounter, a miracle, a loving hand. Love was always near and never far. Your body begins to quake under the weight of sheer amazement you feel. Your head bowed to the sand, your voice joins in the earth's tunes, "Holy, Holy, Holy, is the Lord God Almighty."

You hear each of Love's footsteps move in tandem with the tune. Your eyes watch as the sand dances around you and the words "Holy, Holy, Holy" ring loudly in your ears. The presence of Love grows so heavy that you shut your eyes and see the vibrancy of colors lighting up behind them. The footsteps stop, and the sound of Love's breath begins to fill the air. As He breathes in and out, your breath matches His own. The weight of His presence settles in front of you as Love kneels down. All goes still as Love reaches out His hand and the colors fade to a golden tone. A tear falls from your shut eye, and Love catches it upon His fingertip. The melody fades to a light hum of "Holy, Holy, Holy." You open your eyes and look upon His finger delicately holding your tear, as He places your single tear drop into a small jar and tucks the jar next to His heart.

Love places His hand upon your chin and lifts your head. Your gaze slowly meets His eyes of fire. Not a single thought forms, not a single word comes to mind--you just gaze into His eyes. A warmth fills your body, a peaceful warmth, one you have never felt before. Love smiles, and your heart settles. Love strokes your cheek. "What am I feeling?" you think to yourself. Love smiles knowing your thoughts. "You are feeling Love," He says. Tears of relief fall from your eyes. Love reaches back into His heart and pulls out the small jar. He places the jar filled with a single tear into your hand. Still unable to speak, you wrap your fingers tightly around the jar and look directly into His eyes with a question. He already knows the answer. "The jar with your single tear warmed by my heart is the key." Your gaze leaves His, and you look behind you and see the door still standing tall.

"I don't want to go through that door. I want to stay here in your presence." The thought forms as you bring your attention back to Love. Once again knowing your thoughts, Love responds, "You sat in my presence as your heart removed the chains of rejection, and you experienced my Peace. The pains of this world as arrows were thrown your way, and all the unspeakable loss that you carried for so long was given back to me through Surrender. The long journey through the desert, where you gave up and encountered darkness, gave you an understanding of why you need the light and why you needed to be rescued. You combated the thoughts of doubt and despair by taking one more step without knowing the outcome, allowing the strength of joy to take root in your heart. And now here, under my presence, you fall to your knees in reverence. You see child, you have truly just begun to understand my Love. You have journeyed hard and have realized I am always near and never far; and now with a single tear of complete awe for me, you have gained the key. My presence was with you in it all, even when you didn't feel it. You are always in my presence."

Astounded by what you hear, you lower your head. Love reaches out and brushes the dirt from your breastplate of Righteousness and places His hand on your heart. "Don't hang your head in my presence. You are my child and in you I am well pleased." Your gaze meets His as you feel the jar form into a key within your hand. With a new sense of identity your eyes dance with words of thanksgiving, Love watches knowingly. He stands to His feet and reaches down His hand; you grasp it, and He pulls you to your feet. "It's time to finish the journey but remember..." He pauses and looks at you like a proud papa. You inhale softly. "You are always near and never far," you whisper with confidence. Love smiles and turns with the wind. The sand dances under Love's steps as he disperses into the cloud. You turn back to the door and step forward, placing your hand on the knob. You place the key firmly in the lock and turn it. You push the door open.

Chapter Eleven

Living Stones

You've always given me breathing room, a place to get away from it all. —**Psalm 61:3 TPT**

A sense of resolution renews your passion and gives life to your bones as you push through the unlocked door. The sight is breathtaking: Living Stone Plants cover every inch of earth as far as your eye can see. Vibrant colors of blue and purple mix with subtler colors of pink and yellow. The sight you behold is one of pure radiance. The plants blow gently in the breeze and the detail on each is different than the next. "This could only be the work of the Creator," you think to yourself, as you kneel down and lightly brush a plant with the tip of your finger.

You pick up one in particular that is different from the rest. The outside of the plant is light grey with a webbed pattern of dark grey in the middle. The webbed pattern mimics that of a pair of lungs. The plant itself is a slight moon shape on both sides. The wonder of such a design causes you to gasp and you draw in some fresh air. You gaze at the tiny plant in your hand. As you let the air settle in and out of your body you suddenly feel as if you have breathing room. You are completely surrendered in this moment without a care or a hindrance to limit you, unlike before when you always had a teasing thought of distraction. As you move your eyes from the sweet plant, you gaze to a path that begins to illuminate before you.

You place the plant down in its rightful spot and, with new breath in your lungs, you take your first step on the path as joy fills your body. You glance down at your shoes, those labeled as *The Gospel of Peace*, and smile. Wind whispers, "Share the knowledge of this feeling with everyone you come across." The words from Wind penetrate your heart as you begin to realize this is not a feeling that can be hidden but one that must be shared. As you take your next step your breath becomes heavy in your chest, and you reach up to touch your heart. Once again you feel that familiar breastplate, the one that has only been with you for a short time. It is not as comfortable as your shoes, but it fits perfectly.

Your newfound righteousness surrounds you as a reminder of who you are: you are His and you are Loved. "You have the ability to share the truth of righteousness with those you encounter, and you also have the ability to wound those you encounter further driving them from righteousness." The words of Wind wrap around and ensnare you as a troubled response falls from your lips. "How do I have that kind of power over people?" you ask. "I will show you," whispers Wind.

With a pondering heart, you take another step. The sky is a perfect shade of blue with no desert sand in sight. Living Stone Plants cover every inch of ground as you continue on the path. "I was so consumed with myself and what I needed when I began this journey," you say aloud to yourself, "and now the spiritual things of this world and the people in it seem so much greater..." The half-spoken thought begins to overtake you as you stride down the path, the cool air bringing life to your body as the sun shines brightly above you.

A sense of trust accompanies the joy you feel as you begin to settle in your heart that the journey is not about knowing the answers but embracing the process. As you come around the corner, your ears perk up when you hear familiar shouts in the distance. With a curious spirit you stop and gaze around trying to discern where the sounds are coming from. "Keep going," the words come from within as the shouts become louder. The feeling of hate that you had felt so long ago becomes a resurging reality. "It can't be," you yell out, "I already walked through this hell of a war scene, why this again?" You are desperate for an answer, and that urgency pushes you forward.

You gaze down at your path and notice it is no longer illuminated. The yellow bricks have ended at the base of a hill. Your eyes gaze up at the hill, and the clouds begin to turn in the sky as the wind picks up in strength. The shouts in the distance are recognizable as you muster the strength to take your first step onto the hill. With each step you take you feel Peace returning to your questioning heart. As you reach the top, you gaze down into the valley to see wounded warriors with arrows stuck in their minds and hearts.

This time the warriors are not screaming in agony: they appear to be dead. Hatred fills the air, and the vile smell of witchcraft brews fill your nostrils.

As you watch the atrocious scene before you, you do not feel fear, you feel Peace. "How odd," you think to yourself, "why am I not afraid?" The sky continues to turn various shades of grey as Peace whispers, "Perfect love casts out all fear." A smile spreads across your face then quickly vanishes at the sight you now behold. You muster endurance deep in your heart as you run down the side of the hill and straight into the war scene. The sounds of screeching once again fill your ears and, with a beating heart, you approach a wounded warrior. You kneel next to him with confidence, place your hand around the arrow, and give a tug, "NO!" The words of Wind startle you as your hand goes limp and you look up. "That won't work, you must speak *life*; you must speak righteousness." Confusion crosses your brow. The sky begins to turn to shades of green as the rain falls hard. "I don't know how!" The words fly from your mouth above the noise.

Refusing to give into doubt or frustration, you place your hands on the ground and crawl to the head of your fallen brother. "You are righteous," you whisper in his ear. You gaze over at the arrow deep in his chest. The vile scent coming from the wounds begin to consume your senses as you aggressively gag out the words once again: "You are righteous." You bring your hand to your nose to prevent vomiting and lean back on your heels and stare at the arrow as the minutes pass by.

You bring your attention back to the face of the warrior and suddenly see a small tear fall from the corner of the warrior's closed eyes. The screams go quiet and the smell dormant. You feel a sweet presence settle in next to you, as your eyes move from the tear straight into the eyes of fire. Love catches your gaze, and with a smile, He brushes past you. He leans next to the face of the warrior as He places a jar to his cheek and collects the one fallen tear. Love then places the jar next to His heart. Love kneels close to the ear of the wounded warrior. He begins to whisper, and you lean in close as you hear the words, "No weapon formed against you will prosper." You watch as Love continues to whisper lovingly.

Lost in the moment, you are brought back to your senses as the words "You are loved" are heard. You turn your attention back to the eyes of the wounded warrior and watch as his eyes meet the eyes of fire. A sweet glow forms in them and you recognize it as a glow of identity. Overcome with emotion, you remember the day you said *yes* to Love as the same reflection of fire made space beyond your pupils. A tear falls from your eye as you watch Love gently reach for the arrow wedged in the heart of the warrior and, with a gentle tug, He removes it. The wind begins to blow around the body of the warrior; the color of lavender sweeps in and touches the wounds healing them completely. The process continues until every arrow is gone.

Love stands, reaches down his hand, and grasps the hand of the soldier pulling him to his feet. Love reaches for the jar from His heart and places the jar with a single tear against the chest of the warrior, and a gold breastplate forms. Love kneels and touches the warrior's feet as the shoes of the gospel of peace form. Love stands again and pulls the warrior close into a sweet embrace and then whispers something into his ear. The warrior smiles knowingly and begins to walk in the direction of another wounded warrior.

Arrows fly from every direction towards the healed warrior and the arrows bounce off of his breastplate as he continues in the direction destined for him. Overcome with Peace, you stand. Love turns His attention to you.

You gaze into His eyes as questions fill your mind. "What do you mean that no weapon formed against him would prosper? And why do the arrows bounce off of that warrior?" You point to the healed warrior. The darkness in the distance descends as thunder rolls and lightning strikes. You bring your attention back to Love, and in His presence the chaos is silenced. Above Love's head a colorful rainbow appears. Your mouth drops open; you watch a smile spread across Love's face. His white hair moves with the wind, His face shines with glory, and His white robe is flowing and pure. Love moves towards you, "The healed warrior now knows that he is a son of mine. He is protected, and the false idols of this world no longer cause him to stumble. His breastplate protects him from the arrows that try to pierce him. He mustn't ever take it off." Love reaches out His hand and strokes your cheek. "You spoke life into him; good job my faithful servant."

You bring your hand to your cheek and lay it on top of Love's. Your eyes become misty at the thought of such a simple task accomplishing so much. Love wraps your hand in His and brings His forehead to yours. "You have the ability to share the truth of righteousness with those you encounter, and you also have the ability to wound those you encounter driving them further from righteousness through the power of your words." With your gaze deep in Love's, you squeeze Love's hand tightly. "I can share who You are and speak the truth of your righteousness, or I can spew arrows of hatred from my unhealed pain?" The whispered question comes out more like a statement. A smile spreads across Love's face as He pulls His face from yours.

Love turns from you and walks in the direction of many wounded warriors. The rain begins to soak your body as you slip to your knees. The thunder and lightning cease as the rainbow of Love mixes with a healing rain moving through the battlefield. Your eyes scan the once grueling battlefield of hate and see warriors touched by Love as every arrow is removed from their midst. Your eyes meet those of a fellow warrior who once was dead and is now alive. You recognize the glow in his eyes, a glow of fire, a direct reflection of the fire in Love's eyes.

Your heart fills with comfort as you continue to watch Love roam amongst the warriors accompanied by another being you have not seen before. "Who is that?" you say aloud. "His form comes from Love. He encompasses my *fire*, and the three are one," whispers Wind as he unwraps His presence from yours and hovers over the battlefield once more. The words heighten your senses as you watch this unknown being move amongst the stormy battlefield step in step with Love who brings an ultimate Peace to the hearts He touches.

The scene of the battlefield begins to dissolve before your eyes, as you see an army of angelic forces rise from the hill and invade the area with their presence. They join Love, the unknown being, and Wind, as they touch every heart, remove every idol, and call those who are lost as found. As the last form of light fades, you catch a glimpse of the eyes of the one who is unknown. He stares straight back at you, and you are overcome with a depth of purpose. His eyes are full of radiant colors and dance before you as he gives a slight wink in your direction. A wide smile spreads across His face as you make out the words on His lips: "I choose you." A deep laugh wells up from the pit of your belly as he fades from your sight completely. Overcome with laughter, you fall to your knees and allow your body to sink into the Living Stone Plants once again surrounding you. You take in the fresh air as the plants make way for your body to be engulfed in their wholeness. You slip into eternal security as the words "It has just begun." Fill your soul.

Loved — Study Guide

Soul Expression

Soul Expression is a breakdown of each chapter with correlating scripture of this prophetic journey. This study includes thought-provoking questions to give a deeper and lasting meaning to the essence of an inner healing. Grab your journal and pen as you journey with the Creator of the world through scripture.

Contents

Chapter One

Who is Love?

Section 1:

I chose to introduce God as Love, because scripture tells us:

> **Anyone who does not love does not know God because God is love. In this the love of God was made manifest among us, that God sent his only Son into the world, so that we might live through him. In this love, not that we have loved God but that he loved us and sent his Son to be the propitiation for our sins.** —1 John 4:8-10

What does the word love mean to you?

Do you have a false concept of love?

If so, is that false concept preventing you from accepting what the Word tells us about Love?

Section 2:

I chose this depiction of God because we can only know God if we truly know love. As we grasp the depth of who Love is through the depictions, He shares with us, we soon learn that He knew us before we were formed:

> **Before I formed you in the womb I knew you, and before you were born I consecrated you; I appointed you a prophet to the nations.** — Jeremiah 1:5

God knew you and loved you before you were born—while you were in your mother's womb.

Ask God to show you a time when His love was evident in your life.

Section 3:

Your love for God grows as you realize His deep desire to know you:

> **The Lord your God is in your midst, a mighty one who will save; he will rejoice over you with gladness; he will quiet you by his love; he will exult over you with loud singing.** —Zephaniah 3:17

List three ways you can be intentional about knowing God.

His love for you is so intimate that He even knows the number of hairs on your head:

> **Why, even the hairs of your head are all numbered. Fear not; you are of more value than many sparrows.** — Luke 12:7

What does the word intimacy mean to you?

What would an intimate love of God look like in your life?

Section 4:

The intent of the journey in this book is for us to know God. He knows us, but do we know Him?

> ***I love those who love me, and those who seek me diligently find me.*** —Proverbs 8:17

Ask God to show you how you can seek Him.

As love begins to expose the enemy of our soul, we come to see that the enemy's true character is hatred and his tool is lies:

> ***The thief comes only to steal and kill and destroy. I came that they may have life and have it abundantly.*** —John 10:10

Do you recognize the hate in this world?

Can you tell the difference between what God does and what the enemy does?

Take a piece of paper and draw a line down the middle. On one side write "God" and on the other side write "the enemy." Using scripture as a resource, write down God's characteristics and the enemy's characteristics.

Section 5:

We see God removes fear and anxiety as He calls us to take His hand to begin the journey set before us:

> *...Fear not, for I have redeemed you; I have called you by name, you are mine.* —Isaiah 43:1

Where have fears taken hold of your life?

List your fears, lay them at the feet of Jesus and take His hand to freedom.

Section 6:

You are then introduced to the "eyes of fire" which are mentioned through the entirety of this book:

> *His eyes were as a flame of fire, and on his head were many diadems, and he has a name written that no one knows but himself.* —Revelation 19:12

As you come face to face with Love you are unsure what to feel. He sees the fear in your eyes. So, He introduces you to your companion, Peace, who accompanies you on your journey:

> *Peace I leave with you; my peace I give to you. Not as the world gives do I give to you. Let not your hearts be troubled, neither let them be afraid.* — John 14:27

God did not promise an easy life because we live in a fallen world. He did however promise to leave us His peace. When fear comes, speak "peace be still" over your heart and mind.

List three other ways you can combat fear.

Write a love letter to Love stating your dedication to Him as your Friend.

Chapter Two

My Friend Peace

Section 1:

One thing that might strike you is when Love says, "I am always near and never far." You will find this throughout the chapters:

> ***The Lord is near to all who call on him, to all who call on him in truth.*** —Psalm 145:18

> ***That they should seek God, in the hope that they might feel their way toward him and find him. Yet he is actually not far from each one of us.*** —Acts 17:27

Ask God to show you a time in your life when you knew He was near.

Section 2:

As the journey takes flight you will see that love is constant, but you must take the first step with courage:

> ***Be strong and courageous. Do not fear or be in dread of them, for it is the Lord your God who***

> **goes with you. He will not leave you or forsake you.** —Deuteronomy 31:6

What is the key to being courageous?

Was there a time in your life that you didn't feel courageous and you faced your fear anyway?

When we are in are weakest and fear and anxiety begin to cloud our judgement, we must remember that waiting upon the Lord renews the strength we need to keep going:

> **But they who wait for the LORD shall renew their strength; they shall mount up with wings like eagles; they shall run and not be weary; they shall walk and not faint.** —Isaiah 40:31

In Hebrew the word *renew* means "wait"— wə·qō·w·yê — and is sometimes translated as "hope" but means *wait*.

What does *waiting* on the Lord mean to you?

Do you trust the timing of God?

Do you trust that God is who He says He is according to the Bible?

Section 3:

A common theme throughout the book is signs of anxiety and panic attacks. We are called not to fear, because we have a Father who loves us and saves us:

> **Say to those with an anxious heart, "Be strong; fear not! Behold your God will come with vengeance, with the recompense of God. He will come and save you.** —Isaiah 35:4

Have you ever struggled with an anxiety or panic attack?

What are some ways you overcome these attacks?

Quote this scripture over your fearful heart and command the spirit of fear to leave.

Section 4:

Throughout the book you will see creation rejoicing in reverence to the Lord and many times, the stars and sky are mentioned:

> **All the earth will worship you, and sings praises to you; they will sing praises to your name.** —Psalm 66:4

Spend some time in nature and write down the first three things that God teaches you through His creation.

Only once do you see the word YHWH commonly pronounced as Yahweh. The original word omits the vowels. It is said that when you try to pronounce YHWH without the vowels it sounds like an exhale and then an inhale—the very breath of God in you calls on the name of Yahweh:

> **The Spirit of God has made me, and the breath of the Almighty gives me life.** —Job 33:4

Take a moment of deep breathing and meditate on the breath of God filling your lungs. The very breath of God lives in you.

Section 5:

In the story you experience the chains falling from you:

> **Shake yourself from the dust and arise; be seated, O Jerusalem; loose the bonds from your neck. O captive daughter of Zion.** —Isaiah 52:2

Ask God to show you what chains were holding you down.

Call the chains by name and ask God to give you strength to run free from the chains and lay them down at His feet.

As fear and anxiety turn to despair and hope of continuing on the journey diminishes, suddenly a great shaking takes place on the earth right before the footsteps of Love are heard:

> **And I will shake all nations, so that the treasures of all nations shall come in, and I will fill this house with glory, says the Lord of hosts.** —Haggai 2:7

When things start shaking in our lives, we must look for the footsteps of the Father.

Where is your trust placed when your life gets shaken?

What are three ways you can place your trust in God?

Section 6:

The last words you hear before you march on is "be brave," and we know true bravery only comes by the strength of Him within us:

> ***I can do all things through him who strengthens me.*** —Philippians 4:13

Write a letter to yourself from a place of bravery and courage, encouraging yourself to take a step of faith in your new identity in Christ.

Chapter Three

I Don't Understand Why

Section 1:

We are introduced to a weary traveler questioning how good Love really can be after feeling their efforts have all been for nothing. The greatest love of all was presented in the giving of His son on our behalf:

> **But God shows his love for us in that while we were still sinners, Christ died for us.** —Romans 5:8

Have you ever felt being a follower of Christ was for nothing?

Imagine a God so good that He would send His son to die on your behalf. Is that a love you can trust?

What are three ways you can trust God's process even when you don't understand His plan?

As a traveler, you encountered flowers on your journey. The intensity of their colors is beyond normal observation, and their fragrance and perfection are magnificent. You also absorb the wonder and beauty of the sky and other aspects of nature that are now heightened to your senses. This is evidence of God's love for you:

But, as it is written, what no eye has seen, nor ear heard, nor the heart of man imagined, what God has prepared for those who love him.
—1 Corinthians 2:9

Grab a piece of paper and some colored pencils and ask God to reveal His love for you. Don't take time thinking too much and just begin to draw.

Section 2:

As the reverence for Love becomes undeniable, the deep desire to worship our King can only follow suit:

One thing have I asked of the Lord, that will I seek after: that I may dwell in the house of the Lord all the days of my life, to gaze upon the beauty of the Lord and to inquire in his temple. —Psalm 27:4

What does the word *reverence* mean to you?

Spend some time in reverence to the King with no distractions. List the first three things He teaches you.

Section 3

In Ephesians 6 you will find the entire armor of God and after an encounter with the King you gain your footing fitted with the readiness of the gospel of peace.

What does it mean to have your feet fitted with the readiness of the gospel of peace as Ephesians 6 states?

If you were to share the gospel of peace what would you share?

You have authority wherever the soul of your feet touch. Practice wearing the shoes of the gospel of peace as an activation to the verse shared in Ephesians 6.

Section 4:

Through reverence, you are given the tool of surrender, and with true surrender comes humility. Through this type of surrender you will find gratitude:

Humble yourselves before the Lord, and he will exalt you. —James 4:10

I will give thanks to the Lord, with my whole heart; I will recount all of your wonderful deeds. —Psalm 9:1

As an act of surrender, ask God if there are areas of pride that have taken over your heart.

Lay those places of pride at the feet of Jesus.

List three things you can do if that pride tries to rear its ugly head again.

Section 5:

When we surrender, we leave the baggage of the past behind and walk into the freedom God has for us:

> **Be kind to one another, tenderhearted, forgiving one another, as God in Christ forgave you.**
> —Ephesians 4:32

Many times, the bondage of un-forgiveness weighs us down. Make a list of unforgiveness you are carrying in your heart. Then consider each person and situation and say, "I choose to forgive (insert name or situation) in Jesus' name. It is Finished."

Section 6:

Through the acceptance and knowledge of God and Christ, you can fully put on your new identity leaving your baggage behind and stepping into your identity of son or daughter:

> **But you are a chosen people, a royal priesthood, a holy nation, a people for his own possession, that you may proclaim the excellencies of him who called you out of the darkness into his marvelous light.** —1 Peter 2:9

As a son or daughter loved by a King, write a letter to yourself as if you are writing it to a member of the royal family, stating your excitement of their new position of royalty.

Chapter Four

The Labeled Arrows

Section 1:

The picture unfolds as you first sense an overall weariness, but Peace and Surrender come to the rescue:

> *My flesh and my heart may fail, but God is the strength of my heart and my portion forever.*
> —*Psalms 73:26.*

Name a time you felt completely weary.

What caused that feeling?

How did Peace and Surrender play a part in your recovery?

Section 2:

You instantly become aware of the battle of war as the descriptive scene takes place. We should be prepared for this scene in the spirit realm:

> *Proclaim this among the nations: Consecrate for war, stir up the mighty men. Let all the men of war draw near; let them come up.* —Joel 3:9

Have you ever felt like you were in a war zone?

How did you handle that feeling?

We battle not against flesh and blood by principality and darkness. Our spirit needs to be full of the word of God to defend ourselves against an onslaught of false identity arrows.

As you begin to see the wounded warriors lying lifeless, you realize this is a spiritual battle that has crushed their souls:

> *A joyful heart is good medicine, but a crushed spirit dries up the bones.* —Proverbs 17:22

Ask God to show you places in your soul that are crushed.

Forgive and repent and ask God to cleanse and make right the crooked paths.

Section 3:

Vengeance is the Lord's. Do not take vengeance into your own hands; it will only cause you to grow bitter.

Soon into the battle you realize the wounded warriors succumbed through the venomous shouts you hear in the distance:

> *But no human being can tame the tongue. It is a restless evil, full of deadly poison.* —James 3:8

Are you a person who gossips?

Are your words uplifting or degrading?

What are three ways you can change the way you speak to others?

Section 4:

To depict the sheer evil of this war scene, it is compared to what you would imagine hell to be like:

> **And throw them into the fiery furnace. In that place there will be weeping and gnashing of teeth.** *—Matthew 13:50*

Have you ever been in a situation that felt like how you would imagine hell?

How did you handle that?

Ask God where He was during that hell-like encounter.

Section 5:

The arrows are first labeled as pride which takes root as strife:

> **Insolence comes nothing but strife, but with those who take advice is wisdom.** *—*Proverbs 13:10

Is there strife in your life that has turned to pride because you need to be right?

Do you cause strife in the lives of others because you are broken and need healing?

What are three ways you can end strife in your life and remove the pride that has taken root?

Section 6:

As the labels on the arrows begin to appear, it becomes evident that the hateful words spoken by others' judgments caused labels to take root in the hearts of the wounded warriors:

> *Judge not, that you be not judged. For with the judgment you pronounce you will be judged, and with the measure you use it will be measured to you.* —Matthew 7:1-2

Do you have wounded arrows of judgement piercing your heart?

Ask God to reveal the lies that were spoken over you. For every lie spoken, write the truth of God.

While trying to remove the arrow you are faced with the opposition of a false identity. You realize the wounded warriors have placed their identities in the labels they have accepted instead of what was bought for them on Calvary's Cross:

> *We know that our old self was crucified with him in order that the body of sin might be brought to nothing, so that we would no longer be enslaved to sin.* —Romans 6:6

Write a letter to Jesus letting him know how his sacrifice on the cross has affected and changed your life.

Chapter Five

Love is a Person

Section 1:

As we leave the battlefield, we are overcome with questions for Love mixed with confusion.

> *Likewise the Spirit helps us in our weakness. For we do not know what to pray for as we ought, but the Spirit himself intercedes for us with groaning too deep for words.* —Romans 8:28

Are you wrestling with unanswered questions?

Write three ways you can choose to live in gratitude even while you are processing your questions.

As the rainbow takes your attention, you are drawn to the fact that Love cannot take His gaze from it, as if He is trying to tell you something. The rainbow represents God's promise and the covenant He made with His people:

> *And God said, "This is the sign of the covenant that I make between me and you and every living creature that is with you, for all future generations: I have set my bow in the cloud, and*

> *it shall be a sign of the covenant between me and the earth."*—Genesis 9:12-13

Do you believe you are a part of God's covenant?

What does it mean to have a covenant with the living God?

In your own words, using scripture as a reference and source, write a covenant between you and God and outline His promises to you.

Section 2:

Throughout this entire chapter your thoughts continue to raise the questions of what you experienced in the battle. Isn't this typical of life? Despite the beauty we are surrounded by, and even in the presence of love, our mind still races to thoughts and questions:

> *Do not be conformed to this world, but be transformed by the renewal of your mind, that by testing you may discern what is the will of God, what is good and acceptable and perfect.*
> —Romans 12:2

What does it mean to "conform to this world"?

Ask the Father what ways you have conformed to the things in this world.

Write three ways you can renew your mind when it starts racing with thoughts.

Note: Spending time in God's presence, either in word or worship, always settles a racing heart or mind.

Section 3:

The first time you hear what Love has to share, he says, "My children are so broken and hurting." Many times, we feel that God does not care when our hearts are shattered and wounded, but that is not what His word tells us:

> **The Lord is near to the brokenhearted and saves the crushed spirit.** —Psalm 34:18

Can you think of a time when your heart was broken?

God was close, and His desire is to hold you in those moments.

Envision God in the throne room and allow yourself to run into His arms and climb onto His lap. Lay your head on His chest and listen to the thumping of His heart. Let your broken soul be healed in that place.

In the presence of the Creator, you may be overcome with humility and a feeling of unworthiness, but Love responds by lifting your head. He calls you *worthy*, He calls you *chosen*:

> **But You, O Lord, are a shield about me, my glory, and the lifter of my head.** —Psalm 3:3

Section 4:

The enemy of our soul tries to convince us through lies that we are not worthy in the presence of our Father, but this is not true.

You are called a son or daughter, and He lifts your head to meet His gaze.

What is preventing you from feeling worthy in the presence of God?

Write the words "I am worthy," and recite it to yourself many times each day.

As you realize that you have been seen by God, this opens a new depth of intimacy between you and the Father:

> **See what kind of love the Father has given to us, that we should be called children of God; and so we are. The reason why the world does not know us is that it did not know him.** —1 John 3:1

Do you feel seen and known by God?

Ask God to show you three ways He sees and knows you.

Section 5:

As Love begins to reveal that we live in a world of hate because love is lacking, we then realize we have made idols out of our own accomplishments and have turned those idols into our identity and fear losing them altogether:

> ***And if I have prophetic powers, and understand all mysteries and all knowledge, and if I have all faith, so as to remove mountains, but have not love, I am nothing.*** —1 Corinthians 13:2

> ***Those who pay regard to vain idols forsake their hope of steadfast love.*** —Jonah 2:8

Have you made an idol out of the false identity the world has thrown at you?

Do you fear losing your false identity for fear you will lose everything that is yours?

Ask God to reveal areas of idolatry in your life.

What are three idols you are giving to God?

What are three things He is giving you in return?

> ***The heart of man plans his way, but the Lord establishes his steps.*** —Proverbs 16:9

Section 6:

As you question further about how to remove the idol once you have made it a part of your heart, Love says, "The arrow can only be removed when you let me become a part of your heart. You see child, it is out of relationship with me that you realize there is an arrow, and out of that relationship you have chosen to realize the arrow was never yours to carry. Lastly, out of that relationship you find value and realize the name of the arrow and are given the strength to remove it from your midst. You see child, you need me--Love."

> ***Blessed be the Lord, who daily bears us up; God is our salvation. Our God is a God of salvation, and to God, the Lord, belong deliverances from death.*** —Psalm 68:19-20

> ***Come to me, all who labor and are heavy laden, and I will give you rest. Take my yoke upon you, and learn from me, for I am gentle and lowly in heart, and you will find rest for your souls.***
> —Matthew 11:29-30

> ***And I will give you a new heart, and a new spirit I will put within you. And I will remove the heart of stone from your flesh and give you a heart of flesh.*** —Ezekiel 36:26

What burdens are you carrying that are stopping you from receiving your new heart?

Ask God to remove the idols and give you a new heart.

Out of relationship with God, you realize the idol. Out of relationship with Jesus, you realize that He died to remove the idols and burdens in your life and He carries them for you. And out of relationship with the

Holy Spirit, He the Great Counselor gives you wisdom to name the idol and the strength to remove it.

God is three in one.

Write one way for you to know each person in the *Trinity*.

Only out of relationship with the Trinity does freedom come, and it's your choice to pursue this relationship. God has already made His choice—and it's you!

> **No, in all these things we are more than conquerors through him who loved us. For I am sure that neither death nor life, nor angels nor rulers, nor things present nor things to come, nor powers, nor height nor depth, nor anything else in all creation, will be able to separate us from the love of God in Christ Jesus our Lord...**
> —Romans 8:37-39

Love is a person and peace is a feeling:

> **Peace I leave with you; my peace I give you. Not as the world gives do I give to you. Let not your hearts be troubled, neither let them be afraid. —**
> John 14:27

Write your own guide to what a relationship with God looks like to you.

Ask Him to reveal His unique love to you.

Write what He showed you.

Chapter Six

The Cactus

Section 1:

You soon find yourself in an inner battle of coercion. Many of us find ourselves in the desert season, and even then we should press on and allow God to become even more real to us:

> **It was I who knew you in the wilderness, in the land of drought;** —Hosea 13:5

The moment you realize there is a backpack with supplies, you feel more prepared by what it could contain to get you through the desert:

> **And my God will supply every need of yours according to his riches in glory in Christ Jesus.** — Philippians 4:19

What is a sign that you are in a desert season?

How do you push through?

Christ is in us and He is the hope of glory. He commands us to seek God's kingdom first whenever we feel lost.

Write three ways that God has supplied your needs.

Section 2:

Many times, while we are on our journey we get worn down by the travel, our baggage grows heavy, and the sun grows warm on our backs. During a time when all feels lost and we are defeated, let us not forget that it is God who ordains our paths:

> ***Your word is a lamp to my feet, and a light to my path.*** —Psalm 119:105.

When you are in a time that feels like a quiet season, this is when true dependence upon the Lord is essential. It is helpful to bring gratitude and joy into your life during this time.

Write down a list of things you are grateful for.

Write down a list of things that bring you joy.

What are some uplifting scriptures you can quote when you start to feel low or the baggage is too heavy?

Lay your burdens and baggage at the feet of Jesus.

As we grow weary, we can begin to lose sight of the promises of God. It can feel as if we have been traveling on the journey with no end in sight. People may tell you to snap out of it or choose joy. These are hard feelings when we are going through something that seems to provide no answers:

> *Come to me, all who labor and are heavy laden, and I will give you rest.* —Matthew 11:28.

We all labor, we all struggle, but it was never our job to carry it alone.

What is one way you can choose to lay your burdens at the feet of Jesus daily?

What are some consistent burdens you have carried your whole life?

How are you pursuing help for these issues?

What does *rest* mean to you?

Section 3:

As the mirage of your reality sets in, the defeat from the journey grows heavy. It's important to remember that when all we can see are unchanging circumstances that repeat and seemingly offer no way out, that our Father promises to provide for all of our needs:

> *And God is able to make all grace abound to you, so that having all sufficiency in all things at all times, you may abound in every good work.*
> —2 Corinthians 9:8

God is able and willing. He wants to bless you beyond measure!

Do you struggle with accepting God's desire to bless you?

If so, where is that struggle rooted?

Ask God to reveal His heart to you and remember that God's voice always lines up with His word: it's His basis of truth.

Once you realize God's love for you and His desire for you, then you can't help but abound in every good work.

Section 4:

As the picture of the cactus takes form with its immense height and long spines, it doesn't take long to realize the cactus is you. You have built up a hard exterior with long spikes to protect you from the hurt this world offers. But that hard exterior also keeps love out. It's our job, along with the help of the Holy Spirit, to heal and forgive so our wounds can be cleansed and love can come and make a home as those spikes melt away:

All these evil things come from within and they defile a person. —Mark 7:23

So we do not lose heart. Though our outer self is wasting away, our inner self is being renewed day by day. —2 Corinthians 4:16

But let your adorning be the hidden person of the heart with the imperishable beauty of a gentle and quiet spirit, which in God's sight is very precious. —1 Peter 3:4

What parts of your inner being have become hard and rigid?

What caused those hard parts of yourself to manifest?

Freedom begins when we address our hurts and unforgiveness and take care of our interiors just like our exteriors. God will do a new work for you.

Ask God to bring healing and hope to your broken places.

Who are you choosing to forgive today?

Section 5:

Forgiveness sets us free.

Many times, the weight of our burdens feels too heavy for us to endure, and we distract and try to fix ourselves through our own strength:

> ***The Lord is my strength and my song, and he has become my salvation; this is my God, and I will praise him, my father's God, and I will exalt him.***
> — Exodus 15:2

What areas of your life have you been relying on with your own strength?

What would true surrender in these areas look like?

Imagine Jesus working through these issues alongside you. Ask Him to carry the weight of what you are experiencing; allow the truth of what He has done to be your reality.

Write down ways you find yourself trying to heal your soul through your own strength. Ask God to give you a new strategy on surrendering those things to Him.

Section 6:

The final step of healing from your past trauma and hurts is feeling the pain, and then letting it go into the wind and allowing the Holy Spirit to come alongside you and carry you through the transition of becoming a whole person: Spirit, Soul, and Body:

> ***Let all bitterness and wrath and anger and clamor and slander be put away from you, along with all malice. Be kind to one another, tenderhearted, forgiving one another, as God in Christ forgave you.*** —Ephesians 4:31-32

> ***Let your eyes look directly forward and your gaze be straight before you.*** —Proverbs 4:25

Write a letter to your past self. Write how you are forgiving and moving forward. Choose to see your past self through the eyes of a hurting child, and be patient and kind. Then write a letter to your present self from your past self. Give yourself permission to feel and move on from hurt. Encourage yourself to step into the destiny God has for you and leave your hard exterior of spines behind.

Chapter Seven

The Acacia Tree

Section 1:

You can taste the sand in your mouth and feel the dryness of the journey. However, you feel the freedom of emptying yourself of the past and the possessions that you held close as idols:

> **And he said to them, "take care, and be on your guard against all covetousness, for one's life does not consist in the abundance of his possessions."**—Luke 12:15

What items have you emptied yourself of as you journeyed through this book?

What have you replaced the empty places with?

What things have you made idols of?

Why did I choose the Acacia Tree? The ancient Acacia represents renewal, fortitude, and pureness throughout the world. Some historians believe that the Tree of Life and the Burning Bush of Biblical lore were both Acacia. The scent has qualities of warmth, honey, floral, powder, and balsamic.

Section 2:

Oftentimes we panic and worry about the "what ifs" causing chaos and anxiety. We must lean on His strength overcome this thought pattern.

> ***Casting all your anxieties on him, because he cares for you.*** — 1 Peter 5:7

The knowledge we must remember is that God cares for us even more than we can imagine. All His plans are good plans even if they don't align with our agenda.

Think over the past and write down areas that you were glad God did it His way instead of yours.

Hindsight is 20/20. We must trust the plan God has for us.

Write down three things you are going to trust to God.

Lay those things at his feet, and when the temptation comes to pick up those worries, take a step forward and leave them to God.

Section 3:

As we take a step of faith, encouragement rises and, most times, we must take that step-in spite of our fears:

> ***Keep steady my steps according to your promise, and let no iniquity get dominion over me.*** — Psalm 119:133

God is the one who has the ultimate authority and dominion over us. His word of truth says He has given us authority to tread on serpents. When the fear rings loud, we must take a step of Faith and shout BUT GOD.

What is one area in your life that has frozen you in your tracks?

Ask the Holy Spirit to reveal the truth to you about this situation.

According to scripture, what are God's plans for you?

Step after step, your body tries to get you to stop, your body wants to crumble, and fear shakes you to your core. But you keep going, and then the glorious scent of the Acacia Tree fills your nostrils as you are overcome with peace, and you finally have a chance to quench your thirst and rest. My friends, this is the depiction of God's promises. We must push forward; we must contend with things even when our body is telling us to stop and the fear becomes crippling. God only has the best for us, so we speak, believe, contend, get support from our trusted friends on those extra tough days, and know that God has a beautiful Acacia Tree waiting for us—and it's within our reach by taking that step!

By which he has granted to us his precious and very great promises, so that through them you may become partakers of the divine nature,

having escaped from the corruption that is in the world because of sinful desire. — 2 Peter 1:4

Section 4:

God provides an escape from corruption that can only be attained through the denial of sin, the acceptance of Holiness, and by inviting Jesus to make a home in us.

Have you made Jesus a divine portion in every area of your life? What areas do you want Jesus to come into and cleanse?

Write a letter to Jesus asking Him to cleanse every area of your life and to remove the corruption of sin.

Section 5:

As we close out this chapter, it is important to recognize that God always gives rest to our weary soul and calls us to a place to rest:

In peace I will both lie down and sleep; for you alone, O Lord, make me dwell in safety — Psalm 4:8

How are you learning to rest?

Ask God to teach you how to rest not only in your body but in your soul.

Write down three things that bring your mind rest and practice doing them each week.

Chapter Eight

His Blood is Enough

Section 1:

After a long journey we are always brought back to a season of stillness and a season of peace, allowing our bodies to be still. Chapter 8 starts with a reminder to remember the mission within stillness, and that mission starts with placing the shoes of the gospel of peace back on your feet:

> ***And, as for shoes for your feet, having put on the readiness given by the gospel of peace.***
> —Ephesians 6:15

This type of peace comes from the good news, which is the gospel of Christ that Jesus came to set the captives free. Given the example of shoes, we can't help but take away the fact that we are supposed to spread the good news everywhere that our feet take us.

Are your feet walking in the Shoes of the Gospel of Peace?

What is your definition of the good news?

Ask God three ways you can spread the good news in your life.

Section 2:

As your eyes scan the flowers around you, a certain flower is presented to you: a Golden Sun Cup.

Why a Golden Sun Cup? They are bright, creamy, yellow blossoms with red drops near the centers. Although there are variations, quite often this flower is said to represent joy, youth, purity, happiness, and friendship. It can also mean playfulness, cheerfulness, and sunshine, which reflect the bloom's happy appearance:

> **And calling to him a child, he put him in the midst of them and said, "Truly, I say to you, unless you turn and become like children, you will never enter the kingdom of heaven.** —Matthew 18:2-3

As the stillness continues, I chose to use the image of a Golden Sun Cup flower to represent our need for purity and childlike faith. When we have emptied ourselves of the hindrances that Satan tries to throw at us, we must enter the Kingdom of God with childlike faith.

What does it mean to have childlike faith?

How have you looked to God as a child?

What are three other ways that God is asking you to surrender to him as a child?

Section 3:

The footsteps grow loud as a stoic figure stands before you—one of peace but of demanding stature. You notice first his red cloak and then his sword:

> ***In him we have redemption through his blood, the forgiveness of our trespasses, according to the riches of his grace, which he lavished upon us, in all wisdom and insight.*** —Ephesians 1:7-8

The red cloak represents the power of what the blood of Christ did through the sacrifice of the Father giving His son to the world. Redemption also comes with power and authority as a representation of the power of Christ but also with a sense of peace. Wrap yourself in the cloak of the power of the blood of Christ.

What does the word redemption mean to you?

Who is the person of Redemption?

What does it look like to wrap yourself in the Cloak of the blood of Christ?

Section 4:

As the sword is raised in the air, the words "my blood is enough" become evident, and the power of the very word "redemption" creates a geographical phenomenon.

Why a geographical phenomenon? When lightning strikes sand it creates such an extraordinary event, and the lightning can fuse the sand into silica glass.

This example is given to represent not only the power of the blood but the power of redemption fighting on your behalf. It causes the earth itself to quake at the very thought of that kind of love:

> **And through him to reconcile to himself all things, whether things on earth or things in heaven, by making peace through his blood, shed on the cross.** —Colossians 1:20

What is your understanding of the power of the blood?

Write down three facts concerning a Geographical Phenomenon.

What does this kind of love and redemption mean to your heart and do for your relationship with God?

The Golden Sun Cup flower once again becomes a representation of purity and childlike innocence. The small drop of red in the center is yet another example of the power of the cross:

> **How much more, then, will the blood of Christ, who through the eternal Spirit offered himself without blemish to God, purify our conscience from dead works to serve the living God.**
> — Hebrews 9:14

What do the words: "the blood is enough, it covers your sin, it's your strength, it's your renewal, and it's your beginning" mean to you?

Write an expression of love to God the Father and Christ the Son for his divine example of redemption and the power of the blood.

Section 5:

As the weight of the conversation with Redemption hits you, you are first overcome with surrender and then the feeling of righteousness. Remember the constant power of these two words:

> **Little children, let no one deceive you. Whoever practices righteousness is righteous, as he is righteous.** —1 John 3:7

Surrender any hindrances to the Father as you take on the mindset of a child of faith.

What has God taught you through the character of Redemption?

The renewal takes place as we accept what was done for us at the cross, and the righteousness takes form as we accept ourselves a chosen people, worth dying for, because a Father, a King, a Creator loved us that much:

> **So we do not lose heart. Though our outer self is wasting away, our inner self is being renewed day by day.** —2 Corinthians 4:16

> **Therefore, brothers and sisters, since we have confidence to enter the holy places by the blood of Jesus.** —Hebrews 10:19

Section 6:

We must walk assured as we carry the Breastplate of Righteousness that is rightfully ours through the cleansing of the blood, no longer bound by sin but free to be called a Son or a Daughter:

> **Stand therefore, having on the belt of truth, and having put on the breastplate of righteousness.**
> —Ephesians 6:14

> **Blessed are they who observe justice, who do righteousness at all times!** —Psalm 106:3

Reread the end of Chapter 8 and describe the encounter with Love in your own words.

How will you apply these scriptures in your own life?

Through the scriptures and in your own words, write down what the blood, redemption, renewal, and righteousness mean for your newfound identity.

Chapter Nine

Lion of Judah

Section 1:

Renewed by the character of Redemption, the journey once again begins—such is life. Once again day and nightfall cycle around, and the feeling of discouragement sets in. By now you will have seen a theme: each encounter with Love or a character of Love is followed by a bout of discouragement or fear. This represents our battle of spirit against flesh:

> **We are afflicted in every way, but not crushed; perplexed, but not driven to despair; persecuted, but not forsaken; struck down, but not destroyed.**
> — 2 Corinthians 4:8-9

Have you noticed a theme in your life of discouragement?

Do you expect bad to come after something good has happened?

Ask God to show you what the battle between flesh and spirit looks like.

With each step it appears that even Peace, Surrender, and Redemption have left you. Each of these characters represent the Godhead. When it appears that even the character traits of God have left us when we hit our lowest points, we know it's not true, it's a mere lie of the enemy:

Who is Peace to you?

Who is Surrender to you?

Who is Redemption to you?

Write down how you recognize these within yourself when each is present.

Section 2:

The point and purpose of the journey here on earth can feel clouded and vague at times. When the point and purpose are not within sight, our obsessive need to feel something can drag us to places of displaced longing. In these places we often have the need to feel something we know is not good for us just to escape the feeling of emptiness:

> **Trust in the Lord with all your heart, and do not rely on your own understanding. In all your ways acknowledge him, and he will make straight your paths.** —Proverbs 3:5–6

Only God can show us our purpose and chase those empty feelings away.

Ask yourself these three questions when pursuing your vocational purpose:

What did I naturally do as a child?

What is something that I naturally desire to research or learn more about?

What have my trusted friends and mentors told me I would be good at?

It's important that we don't find our purpose and desire in our vocational calling but in our faith calling, to discern who we are in Him, and from that place will flow rivers of understanding and earthly purpose.

Section 3:

As the reality of the deep numbness and clouded vision grow deeper, we find ourselves in a place of depression with nothing uplifting around us. First, I want to say that if you find yourself in this place, please get help. There is nothing wrong with asking for what you need. We must remember also that Jesus walked through a desert himself, and He relied on faith. When we reach a place of darkness and despair with the numbness of the world eating at our life and future, we must rely on faith to carry us through:

> **Now faith is the assurance of things hoped for, the conviction of things not seen.** — Hebrews 11:1

What is something you have faith in that is unseen?

Seeing is not always believing. Ask God to show you a way out of the dark numbness that has become your reality and to hold tight to the promise of faith.

Darkness and numbness that is left unattended eventually leads to giving up and letting yourself slip emotionally, spiritually, and physically. A sign of giving up can be displayed in many ways which is why the picture of the person slipping into the abyss can display all sorts of ways we give up. The words "When light is absent there is only darkness left" is a play on the scripture:

For without God you are filled with darkness, but a child of God lives as a child of the light. For a split second the person in this story goes towards the light and ends up surrounded in darkness. But once again the glimmer of light comes back, because as Children of light we know He is always near and never far. We can run to the light of the Father.

What areas have you given up spiritually, emotionally, and physically?

How have you let darkness surround you?

What does it mean to run to the light?

Section 4:

As you are pulled back to your senses, the desire to give up grows. You wish to be done, and the weight of that feeling hits you like a ton of bricks. You will then realize the root of this deep desire to be done comes from a root issue called "loneliness." Loneliness causes people to feel empty, alone, and unwanted:

...I have loved you with an everlasting love; therefore I have continued my faithfulness to you. — Jeremiah 31:3

You are loved and wanted with an everlasting love that will never end. You are not alone and never will be when you make Jesus the Lord of your life.

Think back to a time when you were at your loneliest and ask God why you felt He was not there for you.

Section 5:

As the argument with Wind continues you try to give your side of why giving up is a good option, only to find hope lost and desperation setting in. This is a trap and mind game of the enemy. Resist the desire to sink into despair. There is always hope, but you must stand and walk. You must keep going and you will find that hope and support--it's a Promise of God and all His promises are yes and Amen:

Hope deferred makes the heart sick. —Proverbs 13:12

For God gave us a spirit not of fear but of power and love and self-control. — 2 Timothy 1:7

What gives you hope?

What is making your heart sick?

Section 6:

With each step you are restored with hope until the answer comes within sight. Once the answer is in front of you, you can try and rush the process by forcing it open and becoming discouraged once again. But with some encouragement from our companions, little by little the answer is obtained and found in the eyes of the Lion of Judah and the answer brings joy:

> **And one of the elders said to me, "Weep no more; behold, the Lion of the tribe of Judah, the Root of David, has conquered, so that he can open the scroll and its seven seals.** — Revelation 5:5

There is only one permitted to open the scrolls; there is only one who is the author of Creation--and He calls you friend. Run to him in your tired and weary season. Stand and walk. Do not allow numbness or discouragement or hope deferred to stop you from reaching the eyes of the Lion of Judah. Within those eyes you will find the answer, you will find hope, and you will feel again. Through this process, joy will be your strength and will carry you through!

Take time to imagine the fire-filled eyes of the Lion of Judah and write down what you see.

Chapter Ten

The Keys

Section 1:

You come within touching distance of the vibrant Living Stone Plants. How often are the answers we seek within touching distance; when you can feel the excitement as a breakthrough becomes clear.

> *...And who knows whether you have not come to the kingdom for such a time as this?* — Esther 4:14

What has been a moment in your life that you knew you were created for?

What promises are you still holding onto?

As the promise is near we often find a blockage stopping us from going through. In this example I used a door to represent our key to finding a way to break through. Rest assured when faced with a locked door that God always has the key, and He is always near and never far:

What door is blocking your way to your promise?

What does it mean to have the keys of the kingdom of heaven?

Ask God what keys you have been given and what they will unlock.

Section 2:

The earth shouts with a voice of "He's coming" and grows in anticipation as vibrant colors dance and the whole earth rejoices. Our growing anticipation of our King's return should be loudly on our lips as we sing and rejoice with the earth:

> ***Behold, I am coming soon, bringing my recompense with me, to repay each one for what he has done.*** —Revelation 22:12

Do you anticipate the return of the King or are you filled with fear?

Describe in your own words how the world will rejoice when He arrives.

As He comes from the East, His eyes lock with yours, a Father in love with His child. As the presence of Love grows deeper and the earth sings "Holy, Holy, Holy," the impact of seeing your Creator becomes your reality. You begin to realize just who this energy of Love is and how He has always been there through every trial and accomplishment:

> ***There is none holy like the Lord; for there is none besides you; there is no rock like our God.*** —Samuel 2:2

And one called to another and said: "Holy, holy, holy is the Lord of hosts; the whole earth is full of his glory!" —Isaiah 6:3

The Lord our God be with us, as he was with our fathers. May he not leave us or forsake us.
—1 Kings 8:57

Section 3:

Our God is not a man that He should lie. He took on the role of a loving Father in pursuit of you. The earth worships His very name, and yet His eyes are locked with yours. The Creator of the universe was always in step with you, never leaving your side, even when you were unaware of His presence. His desire has always been *you*.

Take a moment to draw a picture of an expression of gratitude towards this reality.

Only through the breath of God can life come to our once empty being. Love is always constant and intimate as He strokes your cheek and lifts your chin. He always places every single drop of tear close to His heart. He sees all and knows all:

By the word of the Lord the heavens were made, And by the breath of His mouth all their host.
— Psalm 33:6

> **You have kept count of my tossings; put my tears in your bottle. Are they not in your book?** —Psalm 56:8

Allow God to breathe life into your broken places.

What places is He breathing life into?

Draw a picture of God collecting your tears.

What does this image mean to you?

Section 4:

Not only does God collect every tear, He knows your every thought, and a love encounter with Him is the key to break through. Through relationship with God all things will be revealed in His timing:

> **We Love because He first loved us.** —1 John 4:19

> **Place me like a seal over your heart, like a seal on your arm; for love is as strong as death, its jealousy unyielding as the grave. It burns like blazing fire, like a mighty flame. Many waters cannot quench love; rivers cannot sweep it away. If one were to give all the wealth of one's house for love, it would be utterly scorned.** —Song of Songs 8:6-7 NIV

Only a love like this can set you free from the depths of yourself.

Love always appears as something. What does this kind of love look like to you?

Section 5:

"You sat in my presence as your heart removed the chains of rejection, and you experienced my Peace. The pains of this world as arrows were thrown your way, and all the unspeakable loss that you carried for so long was given back to me through Surrender. The long journey through the desert, where you gave up and encountered darkness, gave you an understanding of why you need the light and why you needed to be rescued. You combated the thoughts of doubt and despair by taking one more step without knowing the outcome, allowing the strength of joy to take root in your heart. And now here, under my presence, you fall to your knees in reverence. You see child, you have truly just begun to understand my Love. You have journeyed hard and have realized I am always near and never far; and now with a single tear of complete awe for me, you have gained the key. My presence was with you in it all, even when you didn't feel it. You are always in my presence"

It has always been about the journey and what you gain along the way. Peace, surrender, joy, and finally love—each leads to the ultimate prize. This prize is the key which is a love encounter with the One who gave it all to know you! He calls you *friend*; He calls you child; don't hang your head but walk proudly wearing your armor into the place He has called you:

But now thus says the Lord, he who created you, O Jacob he who formed you O Israel: Fear not, for I have redeemed you; I have called you by name, you are mine. —Isaiah 43:1

No longer do I call you servants, for the servant does not know what his master is doing; but I have called you friends, for all that I have heard from my Father I have made know to you. — John 15:15

'And I will be a father to you, and you shall be sons and daughters to me,' Says the Lord Almighty. —2 Corinthians 6:18

Write your testimony and through every twist and turn acknowledge the God who calls you by name, who calls you friend, and who calls you His child. Recall He has been present in every moment.

Chapter Eleven

Living Stones

Section 1:

Why Living Stone Plants? Living Stone Plants are unusual succulents that have evolved to resemble the pebbles and rocks that litter their native habitats. These very small plants hug the ground and grow extremely slowly—it can take years for a plant to fill its pot with new leaves.

I chose these plants to represent the final destination of something so significant and takes years to grow. As we journey with our Father, we are constantly discovering who we are and who He is. This is a long process, but it's always worth the deep beauty that comes out of communing with the Father:

> *Each of you should in the condition in which he was called.* — 1 Corinthians 7:20

Look up information on a Living Stone Plants. What does it mean to you?

Where has God planted you?

Are you blooming—maybe even slowly—where He has planted you?

As you behold the plant that resembles lungs, you realize you have breathing room to just *be*. This is what true surrender looks like, no longer burdened by the pain of the past but completely free, able to breathe in the fresh air:

> *You've always given me breathing room, a place to get away from it all.* —Psalm 61:3 TPT

What does breathing room look like for you?

Ask God to show you how you have gained breathing room through this book.

Section 2:

The Shoes of the Gospel of Peace give you a boldness to move forward and a wisdom-filled endurance to share the good news with every person you encounter. You can no longer hide the light you have found. It must be shared:

> *For to me, to live is Christ and to die is gain.* — Philippians 1:21

> *And he said to them, "Go into all the world and proclaim the gospel to the whole creation."* — Mark 16:15

> *Nor do people light a lamp and put it under a basket, but on a stand, and it gives light to all in the house.* —Matthew 5:13

With knowledge of breathing room, the encounter with Love, and the reminder of the shoes of peace, there is nothing that can stop us from sharing the good news. God equips the saints.

Who is one person with whom you can share the good news of Christ?

Ask God to give you a tangible way to begin the process of sharing what Christ has done for you.

Section 3:

As you grow in your new found righteousness and become comfortable with the idea of being loved and called a child of God, you are presented with the challenge that you can also share this same revelation of righteousness to others—*or* make their journey of finding it more difficult. How? Through the power of your words that you speak to them both directly and when you speak about them with others.

> *Death and life are in the power of the tongue, and those who love it will eat its fruits.*
> — Proverbs 18:21

> *There is one whose rash words are like sword thrusts, but the tongue of the wise brings healing.* — Proverbs 12:18

> *But understand this, that in the last days there will come times of difficulty. For people will be*

> **lovers of self, lovers of money, proud, arrogant, abusive, disobedient to their parents, ungrateful, unholy, heartless, unappeasable, slanderous, without self-control, brutal, not loving good, treacherous, reckless, swollen with conceit, lovers of pleasure rather than lovers of God, having the appearance of godliness, but denying its power. Avoid such people.** — 2 Timothy 3:1-5

Are you driving arrows into your friends and enemies through your words?

Why is the power of your words important?

How can you build those up you love?

How can you pray for those who have hurt you instead of slandering them?

Section 4:

Many of us find ourselves so consumed with what is happening in our lives that we forget to take a moment to look around at Creation and those in it. Take a moment and ask to see the world through Jesus' eyes in order to gain a more authentic perspective of reality. We base our relationship with the Father on how He answers questions. Many times, He answers a question with a question, because we must come outside of our selfish ambition. We need to ask Him what *He* wants to do instead of telling Him what He should be doing for us. This is a trap many people find themselves in time and time again, constantly doubting the goodness of God without ever diving deeper into the truth of His will:

> *A father to the fatherless, protector of widows is God in his holy habitation. God settles the solitary in a home; he leads out the prisoners to prosperity but the rebellious dwell in a parched land.*— Psalm 68:5-6

> *The Spirit of Lord God is upon me, because the Lord has anointed me to bring good news to the poor; he has sent me to bind up the brokenhearted to proclaim liberty to the captives, and the opening of the prison to those who are bound.*— Isaiah 61:1

What if the point of this life is to love God with our whole heart and put others before us unconditionally? What if this belief is truly the essence of our faith calling?

What are your thoughts on these passages?

Write your "Faith Call" statement.

Section 5:

Once again a war scene comes into sight. This is a representation of the warriors who are wounded from the words and idols of the enemy and religion. Afraid to go on, you trust the Wind and move towards it, but this time you only feel peace. When you know who Love is in your life, it casts out fear, witchcraft, and idols. You must stay step by step with Love as you begin a life of ministering to the lost and broken and trust His guidance.

The scene is overrun with defiling words and witchcraft. In a modern context, these are practices involving magic and an affinity with nature, usually within a pagan tradition. Its characteristics are bewitching, fascinating attractions, and charm:

Yet for us there is only one God, the Father, from whom all things and for whom we exist
.— 1 Corinthians 8:6

And my God will supply every need of yours according to his riches in glory in Christ Jesus. — Philippians 4:19

Every good gift and every perfect gift is from above, coming down from the Father of lights, with whom there is no variation, or shadow due to change. — James 1:17

When the war scene was first introduced in Chapter 4, the fear was debilitating. Then in Chapter 11, after walking the journey and experiencing Love's encounter, faith and peace prevail. We can walk boldly now in the knowledge that our Father knows best and, when we walk with Him, He supplies all of our needs. But we have a job to do, and with Him that job becomes obvious.

Have you encountered witchcraft, debilitating fear, or strongholds in your life?

Ask God if there are idols, items, or strongholds in your life that must be removed.

Speak to the fear and introduce it to your Father through faith.

Section 6:

With this knowledge in mind, you approach a wounded warrior and attempt to pull out the arrow. This response is typical of so many of us when it comes to seeing idols or wounds in the lives of those we love. But simply pulling out the arrow will not work, because many people have been living with those arrows for a long time and only a touch from Love can heal the wounds. Our job is to simply speak life and hope into them and pray for them as Love comes and administers the same healing He administered to you when you were wounded. As He collects the tear to heal their wound, He also says, "No weapon formed against you will prosper..."– Isaiah 54:17 this is a promise of God that when we walk with Him through the dark valley, daylight will come and no weapon will prevail:

My help comes from the Lord, the Maker of heaven and earth. — Psalm 121:2

Oh, how abundant is your goodness, which you have stored up for thos33e who fear you and

worked for those who take refuge in you, in the sight of the children of mankind! — Psalm 31:19

Though we are called to minister and spread the good news, we are not called to be our friend's or family's keeper. We must constantly surrender them to God. He is the only one who can remove their arrows and heal their wounds.

Have you been carrying someone you love and trying to pull out their painful arrows?

Write a letter to God surrendering those you love to Him through faith and trust that He will minister to them in His time and in His way.

Ask God to give you a word and prayer to speak over them as you call them to a place of righteousness.

Section 7:

As you watch Love continue ministering to the wounded warrior, He pulls him to his feet and into a position of authority. The once wounded warrior, now healed, walks in the direction of another wounded warrior. The arrows now fling at him, but this time they bounce off of the Breastplate of Righteousness. This is a depiction of the power of knowing who you are, and that only through a relationship with Love will you be equipped and called with this knowledge: "The healed warrior now knows that he is a son of mine. He is protected, and the false idols of this world no longer cause him to stumble. His breastplate protects him from the arrows that try to pierce him. He mustn't ever take it off."

> ***In all circumstances take up the shield of faith, with which you can extinguish all the flaming darts of the evil one.*** — Ephesians 6:16

Our job is to follow the words of our Father, to love the least of these and speak life, then leave the rest in God's hands.

True healing comes from locking eyes with the fire.

Release the controlling spirit that is holding you back from trusting God completely.

Lock eyes with God's Fire-Filled ones. What do you see?

As the wounded warrior locks eyes with Love, his eyes then reflect Love's eye, and he now sees life through the eyes of Love:

> ***Therefore, since we are surrounded by so great a cloud of witnesses, let us also lay aside every weight, and sin which clings so closely, and let us run with endurance the race that is set before us, looking to Jesus, the founder and perfecter of our faith, who for the joy that was set before him endured the cross, despising the shame, and is seated at the right hand of the throne of God.***
> — Hebrews 12:1-2

But my eyes are toward you, O God, my Lord; in you I seek refuge; leave me not defenseless!
—Psalm 141:8

In closing, let us run and finish the race with an endurance filled with faith, keeping our eyes fixed on the perfecter of our soul. The greatest gift you were given was the gift of love--and love has a name-- Father, Great I Am, Protector, Redeemer, Abba, The Alpha and Omega. The divine Creator who breathed life into heaven and earth knows your name and every hair on your head. He is a being who desires nothing more than a relationship with you. He awaits at the door knocking and hoping for a chance to dine with you. He is the lover of your soul, the one who heals all your wounds and breathes life back into your dry bones, the one who performs miracles and calls those dead to come alive. He desires you. Run to Him, let love in, let love reign, and pursue it with a passion-filled anticipation until the return of the savior of the world. All this is commissioned by a Father who longs to stroke your face and gaze into your eyes with a love our earthly minds cannot even begin to comprehend.

Coming Soon...

Chosen

Hello my friend, my eyes dance with color as I look into your eyes, and my Spirit is wild about you. Allow me to introduce myself, I Am the Redeemer. I was chosen by my Father to take the place of pain so you would not have to. My Spirit is one with the Father's and my mind is set on the things above. When I was in the world I was not moved by the things of this world. I know the temptations of sin, as I too was once tempted. I have seen what pride does to a man as I once called out sin through stories of long ago. I Am alive and real. Stories of me have been told throughout the pages of history, they were not fairytales as one may suppose, they were real.

I came to redeem the world and set the example for the life I have called you to live. We are not as different as you may think, in fact our DNA crosses through time as we are both called a child of God. My love for you is deep and wide like that of my Father's and I understand your struggles and pain, as I too cried out to Father to deliver me from pain. Friend, I became flesh so that what sin stole could be reclaimed. What was once missing is now found in a relationship with me. I crossed the barrier so you can commune with Father. Sin has been defeated and death has been claimed. I have come to give you life and life more abundantly. I was the first and I Am the last. Through union with me, you too will discover what it means to be set apart. The world hated me, they too will hate you, but my friend, it will be worth it.

Apart from anything else I ask that you remove your walls you have set against me and allow my kindness to crawl into your heart. I know the world has left you dry and defeated. I know you have been rejected and spit on. My friend, I know this because the world rejected me too. My love is not tainted, in fact I died for those who rejected me. I gave my life for those who spit in my face, and I would do it all over again. My blood that was spilled on your behalf and has the power to set you free from your pain and tormenting thoughts. It also has the power to replace what was lost as you find the answers you long for.

I Am kind, patient, and good. I am also fun. I want to add some joy back to your life as you dream and imagine with me. I will add wisdom to your life as I transform your dry heart to one heaping with compassion. My word outlines my desire to walk with you as I disciple you in the ways of my strategic wisdom. Break me out of the box you have put me in Friend, I have much to show you.

Let's continue on the journey that you started with Love not that long ago. In my presence there is no man-made time, just a union of richness to be explored. Take my hand as we journey back through the mind and into the imagination where your creativity lives and where I become alive.

ABOUT
KHARIS PUBLISHING

KHARIS PUBLISHING is an independent, traditional publishing house with a core mission to publish impactful books, and channel proceeds into establishing mini-libraries or resource centers for orphanages in developing countries, so these kids will learn to read, dream, and grow. Every time you purchase a book from Kharis Publishing or partner as an author, you are helping give these kids an amazing opportunity to read, dream, and grow. Kharis Publishing is an imprint of Kharis Media LLC. Learn more at
https://www.kharispublishing.com.

CPSIA information can be obtained
at www.ICGtesting.com
Printed in the USA
FSHW020430060621